PRESIDENTS OF THE UNITED STATES OF AMERICA

A HISTORY OF AMERICA'S LEADERS

FRANKLIN TAYLOR

ROHRER
PUBLISHING

© **Copyright 2020 - All rights reserved.**

The content contained within this book may not be reproduced, duplicated or transmitted without direct written permission from the author or the publisher.

Under no circumstances will any blame or legal responsibility be held against the publisher, or author, for any damages, reparation, or monetary loss due to the information contained within this book. Either directly or indirectly. You are responsible for your own choices, actions, and results.

Legal Notice:

This book is copyright protected. This book is only for personal use. You cannot amend, distribute, sell, use, quote or paraphrase any part, or the content within this book, without the consent of the author or publisher.

Disclaimer Notice:

Please note the information contained within this document is for educational and entertainment purposes only. All effort has been executed to present accurate, up to date, and reliable, complete information. No warranties of any kind are declared or implied. Readers acknowledge that the author is not engaging in the rendering of legal, financial, medical or professional advice. The content within this book has been derived from various sources. Please consult a licensed professional before attempting any techniques outlined in this book.

By reading this document, the reader agrees that under no circumstances is the author responsible for any losses, direct or indirect, which are incurred as a result of the use of the information contained within this document, including, but not limited to, — errors, omissions, or inaccuracies.

GEORGE WASHINGTON
1ST PRESIDENT OF THE UNITED STATES, 1789-1797

George Washington has been called "first in war, first in peace, and first in the hearts of his countrymen."

Washington was born on February 22, 1732, in Pope's Creek, Virginia. His nickname was "Father of His Country."

Washington had a pivotal role in shaping the job of the president and with it the future of the new nation.

He realized this and once said, "I walk on untrodden ground. There is scarcely any part of my conduct that may not hereafter be drawn into precedent."

He grew up the son of a prosperous farmer in Virginia. When he was eleven, his father died, and he went to Mount Vernon to live with his older half-brother, Lawrence. He had off and on schooling but was always naturally good with numbers. When he was just fourteen, he surveyed his father's farm just for fun. When he was twenty, his brother Lawrence died, and Washington became the owner of Mount Vernon.

At twenty-one, he joined the military. He eventually rose in the ranks and became commander of all the Virginia troops and led them in small battles against the French as well as against the Native Americans. At twenty-six, he decided to quit the army and settle down with a widow named Martha Dandridge Custis. He spent the next 15 years as a wealthy tobacco farmer on his farm Mount Vernon.

Times were changing quickly in the American colonies, which at the time still belonged to England. Many Americans thought they were being mistreated and deserved to have more say about their government, rather than be ruled by a foreign leader. The tension eventually grew into what we now know as the Revolutionary War. On April 19, 1775, British soldiers met in battle against American forces at Lexington and Concord. Due to Washington's military experience, he was appointed commander-in-chief of the American army. Washington was the perfect fit, not only because of his military knowledge, but also because he was wealthy, and Congress could not afford to pay him.

Military experts reflect that Washington was a capable general. His armies had their fair share of losses, but they were never destroyed or captured. Washington knew that as long as the Americans could keep an army on the field, the British would not win. This is where he excelled as a leader; it was his unique ability to inspire men. His soldiers did not have enough guns or ammo and were often tired and hungry, yet they still fought for him because Washington never left their side. He fought and suffered with his men, and they felt as long as he was their leader, they could not lose.

Eventually, America won the war, and the colonies became free and independent states. After a time, the states considered themselves independent and started to quarrel. In 1787, men from the different states met in Philadelphia to try to arrange a new government. This was called the Constitutional Convention. Many of the most influential men in

America attended. Washington was elected chairman of the convention, and his job was to hold it together, as he had held his army together. Eventually, they drew up the Constitution of the United States of America. It called for a strong central government headed by a president. Washington was unanimously elected and became the first President of the United States of America (USA or U.S.).

Washington believed that as the chief officer of a new nation, he should present a dignified appearance, similar to that of a king. Washington dressed very formally and was pulled by fancy carriages with beautiful horses to keep up his appearances.

In 1793, Washington was elected to a second term right as the nation was facing new problems. He worked tirelessly to keep the U.S. out of the ongoing European war between France and England. However, he was still willing to use military force on U.S. soil. One of his first great tests as leader of the nation was the Whiskey Rebellion.

In March of 1791, Congress created a tax on whiskey that angered farmers who made whiskey from the extra corn they grew. In July of 1794, federal agents in Pennsylvania tried to collect the whiskey tax. Still, the farmers rebelled and refused to pay. The Pennsylvania governor failed to enforce the law and collect the tax, so this turned into a federal problem.

This was a direct challenge to the newly formed American government and their authority. This prompted Washington to raise a volunteer army and enforce the law himself. Although it never posed a severe threat of war, this was a pivotal moment for the newly formed government. By putting out the Whiskey Rebellion, Washington proved that the federal government had the power to enforce its laws.

Most people wanted him to be president for a third term, but at sixty-five years of age, he was tired. He refused a third term and retired back to the life he enjoyed at Mount Vernon. However, it was short-lived. On December 12, 1799, while traveling through a snowstorm, he became sick, and two days later, he died. The news of his passing came as a great shock to the whole world. Even the British, whom he had fought against, had learned to admire and respect him. Thomas Jefferson, who often disagreed with Washington politically, said, "He was indeed in every sense of the words, a wise, a good, and a great man."

JOHN ADAMS

2ND PRESIDENT: 1797 TO 1801

Born on October 30th, 1735, John Adams grew up on a farm in Braintree (now Quincy), Massachusetts, where he spent much of his time hunting in the woods. He graduated from Harvard and became a lawyer in Boston. From 1774 until 1777, Adams served as a Massachusetts delegate to the Continental Congress in Philadelphia. There, he nominated George Washington to be commander-in-chief of the Continental Army. He also assisted Thomas Jefferson in composing the Declaration of Independence. During the Revolutionary War, he served as a diplomat for the colonies in France and Holland. He even helped negotiate peace at the war's end. He was the first U.S. diplomat to England and returned in 1788 to serve as Washington's vice president.

Adams was not happy in his job as vice president. He wanted to be engaged with the actions of the office, but as vice president, he wasn't afforded that luxury. While in office, he once wrote to his wife that the job of vice president was "the most insignificant office that ever the invention of man contrived."

Adams had expected to succeed Washington as president. Still, he only won by a small margin over his political foe, Thomas Jefferson, who became vice president. Like Washington, Adams did not believe in political parties. Unfortunately for Adams, political parties had been formed, and he soon found himself in trouble.

The most critical problem facing John Adams when he took office was French raiding American shipping. Both Great Britain and France were at war with each other and desperately wanted supplies from the United States. Neither was willing to let the other side receive goods and would raid American ships that were trying to deliver supplies to their opposition. As the raids increased on the American merchant ships, Americans began demanding war on France. Remembering the warning against foreign powers delivered by Washington in his farewell address, Adams decided against it. The United States was not yet able to fight at sea, and it would take years to build a Navy. He asked Congress to order new warships. This led to a navy department being established for the first time. Adams is sometimes called the "Father of the United States Navy." The first ship in the fleet was the 44-gun *United States*. This was followed by the 36-gun *Constellation* and the frigate *Constitution*, later nicknamed "*Old Ironsides*." There was no declaration of war, but French and American warships fought whenever they met.

During this time, Adams obtained passage of the Alien and Sedition Acts. These laws made it hard for the Democratic-Republicans to organize opposition to the government. Thomas Jefferson publicly accused Adams of signing these laws in order to frustrate his political adversaries. Over the next year, ten newspaper editors were thrown in jail under the Sedition Acts. Thomas Jefferson and James Madison wrote the Kentucky and Virginia Resolves, which argued that the new laws were void because they were unconstitutional. This argument would become much more critical in the years leading up to the Civil War.

Near the end of Adam's term as President in 1800, the government moved from Philadelphia. The Adams' became the first presidential family to live in the muddy, new capital of Washington, D.C., where the White House was only partly finished at that time. The campaign of 1800 was very similar to the election of 1796 between Adams and Jefferson, a bitter one. Adams lost the election of 1800 to Thomas Jefferson.

Although the end of his presidency was turbulent, Adams enjoyed retirement at his home in Massachusetts. He spent most of his time reading books in his library. He would often have his eighteen grandchildren, and great-grandchildren read to him when his sight failed. As time passed, he even renewed his friendship with Thomas Jefferson. At eighty-nine, Adams was able to witness his son John Quincy became the sixth president of the United States. Two years later, he was invited to participate in Boston's celebration of the fiftieth anniversary of the Declaration of Independence. Adams never made it, however, passing away on July 4, 1826. His last words were, "Jefferson still survives." He had no way of knowing this, but Jefferson had died only a few hours earlier that night at his Monticello estate in Virginia.

THOMAS JEFFERSON
3RD PRESIDENT: 1801-1809

Thomas Jefferson was born on April 13, 1743, in Albemarle County, Virginia. His parents were well-to-do in the Piedmont region of the Commonwealth of Virginia. Jefferson grew up with a sharp mind, studying multiple languages, law, mathematics, science, and philosophy. He was known as a renaissance man because he held such a range of interests, one of which, was architecture. When the government held a competition to design the president's new home, Jefferson submitted a design anonymously, but unfortunately, he did not win. However, he did design his own house named Monticello located right outside of Charlottesville, Virginia.

At twenty-six, Jefferson was elected to the Virginia Legislature. Jefferson was not a strong public speaker, so he would often write letters and articles to convey his thoughts. The subjects of these letters centered mostly on the impending trouble between the colonies and Great Britain. Jefferson grew in popularity as these articles began to circulate. His opposition to England became so strong that the British declared him a traitor and ordered that he be hanged as soon as he was captured.

In 1775 he was appointed to write the Declaration of Independence. When the new Constitution was adopted, and Washington was elected president, Jefferson was appointed the secretary of state. He believed that people should and could govern themselves. He believed that only educated citizens could safeguard the new democracy. Alexander Hamilton, Washington's secretary of the treasury, did not agree with Jefferson's ideas on government. He believed that the English system, headed by a king or at least a lifetime president, would be best. Their differences led to the formation of the country's first political parties. Jefferson soon became the leader of the Republican Party, which years later would change their name to the Democratic Party. The men who agreed with Hamilton became known as Federalists.

When Washington refused to serve a third term, John Adams was elected president, and Jefferson became vice president. John Adams belonged to the Federalist Party and Jefferson to the Republican party. This happened because the men who wrote the Constitution had not thought about political parties. They planned for the man who got the most votes to be president and for the man who got the second most votes to be vice president. Later the Constitution would be changed so that the president and vice president would always belong to the same political party.

Adams served only one term before Jefferson was elected 3rd President of the United States. John Adams did not remain in Washington to see Jefferson's inauguration on March 4, 1801. Jefferson did not wear handsome uniforms or ride in fancy carriages pulled by many horses as Washington once had. Instead he typically walked or rode on horseback.

Jefferson concentrated on making the federal government smaller and less involved in the daily lives of the people. He reduced the size of the military, recalled more than half of the American Diplomats in Europe, and ordered a review of government spending. In time, these measures reduced the national debt by about one-half.

During Jefferson's presidency France and England were still at war. Jefferson feared that France might try to deny Americans the right to travel up and down the Mississippi River, which would decimate trade on the western frontier. The people settling the Mississippi River countryside at this time were mostly poor farming families. The only land these people could afford was on the untamed western frontier. They would usually travel west on foot, carrying their belongings on their backs. Once they found a place to settle, they would build log cabins. Jefferson believed farmers were the key to a stable and productive nation, and he wanted to be sure that they could ship their goods to market down the Mississippi River.

In 1803, Jefferson tried to buy New Orleans from France. To his surprise, Napoleon, the French emperor, offered to sell the whole Louisiana territory, from the Mississippi River to the Rocky Mountains. The problem was that nothing in the Constitution said that the president had the power to double the size of the United States. Jefferson was conflicted because he believed that the future of the

United States lay in the west but to obtain that land he would be expanding the reach of the federal government's power. He had to compromise to make the Louisiana Purchase, but the offer was too good to pass up. The irony for Jefferson was that the purchase also ensured the need for a strong central government to manage the vast new country.

Before he approved the Louisiana Purchase, President Jefferson sent an expedition to explore the Louisiana Territory. He asked his personal secretary, Meriwether Lewis, to lead the exploration. Lewis wrote to William Clark, a veteran soldier, asking him to become co-leader of the expedition. On May 14, 1804, Lewis and Clark left St. Louis accompanied by thirty soldiers and ten civilians, including experts in zoology, sign language, botany, and navigation. Later, they took on a fur trapper Charbonneau and his Shoshone wife, Sacajawea, to help them communicate with the Native Americans. The explorers sailed up the Missouri River into what is now North Dakota. On November 7, 1805, the expedition reached the Pacific Ocean. Both Lewis and Clark made maps and kept journals of their trip across the continent. The journals provided an enormous amount of new scientific information about the country's landscape.

In 1804, Jefferson was elected for a second term. France and England were still at war. English warships often captured American merchant ships to keep them from trading with France. To avoid war, Jefferson got Congress to pass a law forbidding American ships to trade with either England or France. He believed that withholding U.S. goods would force both France and Britain to respect U.S. neutrality. He signed the resulting Embargo Act in December of 1807. However, it was a disaster, hurting Americans much more than it did the British or the French. Without European buyers, many U.S. crops simply rotted away in storage, and thousands of people in the shipping business lost their jobs. A year later, Congress passed a bill repealing the embargo, which Jefferson reluctantly signed on March 1, 1809, three days before leaving office.

Jefferson might have been elected again if he had wished but he was afraid that if a president served for too long, he might be tempted to become a dictator. He believed the president should serve no more than two terms. Jefferson went back to Monticello and to his life as a plantation owner. Like other plantation owners, Jefferson was a slave owner. He was troubled by slavery, and in his will, he freed his slaves, but only after he died because he did not want to seem to be criticizing his slave-owning neighbors.

After his presidency, Jefferson planned and helped build the University of Virginia. He brought together teachers and helped decide what subjects should be taught. Thomas Jefferson died on the same day as John Adams, July 4, 1826. It was exactly fifty years after the Declaration of Independence, which he had written. Jefferson wrote the words to go on his gravestone: "Here was buried Thomas Jefferson, author of the Declaration of Independence, of the Statute of Virginia for religious freedom, and father of the University of Virginia." He did not even mention having been President of the United States.

JAMES MADISON

4TH PRESIDENT: 1809 - 1817

James Madison was born in Port Conway, Virginia. He was a thin and sickly child who never weighed much more than a hundred pounds and was only five foot four inches tall. As he grew older, his health improved, and he attended Princeton University, where he graduated in only two years. For a time, he considered being a preacher since he was deeply religious and was passionate about religious freedom. He thought religion and government needed to be kept completely separate. Instead of going into seminary, Madison went into politics.

During the Revolution, he served in the Continental Congress. Madison knew that if the country was to grow, it must have a powerful central government.

He and other leaders urged that a convention be called to form such a government. This convention finally met in Philadelphia in 1787. This is where the Constitution of the United States was written. Due to his leadership during this time, Madison is often referred to as the 'Father of the Constitution.'

When the new government was formed, Madison was elected to the House of Representatives. There he led the fight to add the first ten amendments to the Constitution. These are known today as the Bill of Rights.

In 1801, Thomas Jefferson appointed James Madison Secretary of State, where they worked closely together for eight years. When Jefferson retired, Madison was elected the 4th President of the United States. Madison inherited a country in crisis. The Embargo Act had just been repealed, but its negative effect on the U.S. economy was still being felt. France and Britain were not any closer to respecting U.S. neutrality at sea.

Low on options, Madison signed into law Macon's Bill Number Two, which said that if either Britain or France agreed to respect U.S. neutrality, the United States would cut off trade with the other nation. Napoleon was willing to accept this on behalf of

France, so Madison re-imposed the trade embargo on Britain.

During the midterm elections of 1810, voters replaced nearly half the members of Congress with much younger politicians who promised to end the nation's ongoing humiliation. These new congressmen were known as War Hawks because if they were elected they promised to declare war on Great Britain. With all of this new pressure on Madison, he finally gave in and asked Congress for a declaration of war.

The War of 1812 turned out to be much more difficult to win than first anticipated. Unwilling to challenge the powerful British navy at sea, Madison focused on a land campaign against British Canada. The best invasion routes passed through New York and New England, but none of these states would permit an attack across its border since they opposed the war. Because of this, the first attack on Canada was launched from Detroit in July of 1812. Madison unwisely chose an aging revolutionary war veteran, William Hull, to lead the charge. General Hull crossed the border, but due to his fear of a Native American attack, quickly withdrew back to Detroit. He then surrendered to the lesser British army without ever firing a shot. For his cowardice, Hull was court-martialed.

James Madison was elected for a second term in office in March of 1813. The country was still in crisis as the plan to invade Canada had failed, and now the British were on the offensive. In December, British forces crossed the Canadian border into the U.S. and burned Buffalo, New York. Eight months later, they swept past weak U.S. defenses in the Chesapeake Bay and marched on Washington, burning the Capital on August 24, 1814.

When the British attacked Baltimore during the War of 1812, they had a prisoner aboard one of their ships named Francis Scott Key. From his vantage point, Key was able to witness the British bombardment of Fort McHenry during the night of September 13-14, 1814. The British kept up the attack throughout the night, and Key witnessed the horror. At dawn, Key strained to see whether the U.S. flag was still flying above his fort. His joy at seeing the Stars and Stripes inspired him to write "The Star-Spangled Banner." The song became the official national anthem in 1931.

In January of 1814, the British had informed President Madison that they were prepared to discuss terms for peace. Madison immediately jumped at the chance and sent a delegation to meet with the British at a neutral site. Great Britain had better things to do than continue fighting a war an ocean away. Eventually, the Treaty of Ghent was signed in December. Neither side gained or lost any territory, and other matters such as neutrality rights of U.S. shipping were left unresolved. The treaty did have a lasting effect, however, in that it brought closer relations between the two countries. After the war, Britain showed a great deal more respect to the United States than it ever had before.

Unfortunately, while the Treaty of Ghent was being negotiated, the war continued. The last battle was fought on January 8, 1815, two weeks after the signing of the treaty. This was because it took much longer than two weeks for news to travel across the ocean. At the end of his second term, Madison was glad to retire and go back to his home in Virginia. He was president during a challenging time. Some have said that his greatest professional achievement was writing the Constitution. He played a significant role in designing the system of checks and balances in the U.S. government. He created the idea of a presidential veto and a judicial branch that could override state laws.

Madison did not get married until he was forty-three years old. He was much older than his bride, Dolley Todd. Dolley Madison was known for her charm and intelligence, which is why she stands out as one of the nation's most extraordinary first ladies. During the War of 1812, she proved that she could remain poised under crisis. In August of 1814, Dolley was planning a dinner party for forty guests when the British closed in on Washington. The president was already safely out of town, and now his wife was told to flee for safety. Before she did, she grabbed the Declaration of Independence, the national seal, a portrait of George Washington and her pet parrot. She sent them ahead of her for safety. After her husband's death, she returned to the capital and again took up her position as the leading lady of Washington society.

JAMES MONROE
5TH PRESIDENT: 1817 - 1825

Like all the presidents before him, except John Adams, James Monroe was born in Virginia. His father died when he was about sixteen years old, at which time he inherited all of his family's property. He left home to go to William and Mary College. His mind wasn't on his studies, and like most students at William and Mary at the time, he was caught up in the patriotic fever sweeping the colonies. In March of 1776, he dropped out of college and enlisted in the Continental Army. After the war, Monroe studied law under Thomas Jefferson. Although Jefferson was fifteen years older than Monroe, the two men became very close friends. When Monroe was only twenty-four, he was elected to the Virginia legislature. He later served in the U.S. Senate and also as governor of Virginia.

In 1811, President James Madison appointed Monroe Secretary of State. For a while during the War of 1812, Monroe served as both Secretary of State and Secretary of War. In 1816, James Monroe was elected as the 5th President of the United States. By then, the war of 1812 was over. The British had burned the president's house so thoroughly, that it still wasn't habitable when he was sworn into office. Rather than living in temporary housing, Monroe decided to take a tour of the country until the work on the house was completed. He wanted to have an up-close look at the country he would be in charge of.

He began his tour in Washington, and he traveled north, all the way up to Maine. From there, he turned west to Detroit and then southeast, back toward Washington. He traveled over 2,000 miles on his tour route and was the first president to ride a steamboat (from Baltimore to Philadelphia) and the first sitting president to travel as far west as Michigan. The trip took fifteen weeks and gave Monroe a much more in-depth knowledge and understanding of the country. People remembered that he had been an officer in the Revolution and wounded in battle. Everywhere he went, he was met with cheers and large crowds. One Boston newspaper described Monroe's reception as the beginning of an "era of good feelings" for the country.

Even though the war was over, both the United States and Great Britain still had warships on the Great Lakes. There was always a chance that fighting might begin again at any time. Monroe suggested that each country limit its warships on the lakes to a few very small ones. England complied, which set up a spirit of friendly cooperation that still exists between the United States, Great Britain, and Canada to this day.

Former War Hawks, Henry Clay and John C Calhoun brought forth a series of projects designed to improve the country's infrastructure, such as its roads, bridges, and canals. These projects became a series of bills proposed to Congress called the American System. One of these bills imposed a tax on manufactured goods being imported into the country. This tax made European goods more expensive to buy, which encouraged Americans to purchase locally. The money raised by the taxes would be used to build roads and canals in the western territories.

Monroe agreed this would be beneficial but, at the same time, feared that this type of project went well beyond the powers granted to the federal government. Monroe eventually vetoed the bill because he believed road building was the responsibility of the states. It was the only bill that Monroe vetoed while in office.

During Monroe's administration, the country grew at a rapid pace. Between 1816 and 1821, six new states joined the Union (Maine, Mississippi, Alabama, Illinois, Missouri, and eventually Florida), making a total of twenty-four United States. They were generally welcomed in the South and in the West but these states unsettled some Americans in the North. Those in the North knew that as the country expanded, their needs would be less critical. Northern factory owners wanted higher taxes on imported manufactured goods while also wanting raw materials to remain cheap. In the West, farmers wanted the exact opposite. They wanted to receive high prices for the raw materials they grew and be able to pay low prices for the factory goods they bought. In the South, plantation owners were concerned about slave labor changing, which would hurt their ability to produce cotton at a competitive price.

The balance of power was a significant concern for the North and the South. Many northerners wanted to get rid of the brutal institution of slavery, which the South relied upon. Both sides knew that the key votes on slavery would be cast in the West. If the new western states were admitted as free states, then slavery would most likely go away, even in the south. In the thirty years since the Constitutional Convention, the cotton gin had made the South even more dependent on slave labor. To preserve this, Southerners demanded its extension to the new western states.

This issue came to the forefront in 1819 when Missouri applied for statehood. Everyone wanted to know if Missouri would be a slave state or a free state. In Washington, Congress debated whether the federal government had the power to ban slavery in the new states. Congress debated for some time without making a decision until Maine wanted to join the Union. Being so far north, Maine would most likely be admitted as a free state. With that in mind, a compromise was made; Maine and Missouri would be admitted together. Maine as a free state and Missouri as a slave state. What made the deal work was that the southerners also agreed to a northern demand that slavery be banned in the rest of the Louisiana Territory north of the latitude 36 degree 30'. This was known as the Missouri Compromise. Monroe considered vetoing the Missouri Compromise, but he suspected that a veto would likely lead to civil war. He signed the Compromise on March 6, 1820.

Monroe was elected to a second term later that year and received every vote in the electoral college except one. The one man who voted against Monroe said he did not think anybody but George Washington should ever get all of the votes.

Monroe's time in office saw little issues along the western frontier. He did face a problem in Georgia, where the Seminoles and American settlers began killing one another in large numbers. Seminole raiding parties, which included runaway slaves, burned the farms of American settlers whom they believed were stealing their land. Most of the Seminoles lived in Florida, which was still a colony of Spain at the time. Both the Seminoles and Creeks helped escaped slaves because they shared the mutual hatred of the American settlers.

In 1817, Monroe sent Andrew Jackson, the county's most capable general, to punish the raiders. Jackson's hatred of the Native Americans was well known, and he used these attacks as an excuse to invade Florida. He then captured the Spanish stronghold of Pensacola, which gave him control of northern Florida. Although Jackson didn't technically disobey his orders, his decision to invade Florida was not sanctioned by the Monroe administration. The Spanish minister demanded that Jackson be punished, but Secretary of State John Quincy Adams defended Jackson and used Jackson's presence as a negotiating tool with Spain. Adams demanded that Spain either control the Seminoles or transfer control of the territory immediately to the United States. With General Jackson's army already in place, Spain decided to sell all of their land east of the Mississippi River as well as its claim to the territory of Oregon for five million dollars.

Now that the U.S. controlled so much of North America, John Quincy Adams suggested to President Monroe that he warn Europe against any further colonization of the Western Hemisphere. On December 2, 1823, Monroe delivered a speech to Congress outlining what soon became known as the Monroe Doctrine. This was a statement of policy that has guided U.S. actions ever since.

When Monroe's second term was over, he went back to his home in Virginia. He became regent at the University of Virginia and presided at the Virginia Constitutional Convention of 1829. He died while visiting his daughter in New York on July 4th, 1831. Of the five Presidents who took part in the Revolution, three of them -- John Adams, Thomas Jefferson, and James Monroe - all died on the Fourth of July.

JOHN QUINCY ADAMS
6TH PRESIDENT: 1825 - 1829

John Quincy Adams was the son of John Adams, the second President of the United States. John Quincy Adams was only seven years old when the Battle of Bunker Hill was fought, and it was a day he would never forget.

When John Quincy Adams was eleven years old, his father moved to France to become an American diplomat. He took his eldest son with him. Over the course of the next few years, he went to school in France and Germany. When he was only fourteen, he served as secretary for the American minister in Russia. He then worked as a secretary for his father. During this time, John Adams helped write the peace treaty that ended the American Revolution.

When the fighting ended, John Quincy Adams attended Harvard University, where he graduated in 1787 and began to study law. Soon he was sent by President Washington to represent the U.S. in many different European countries.

When Thomas Jefferson became president, John Quincy Adams returned to the U.S. and was elected to the Senate as a member of the Federalist party. Similar to his father and George Washington, he did not believe in political parties. Adams voted for what he thought was right, not what the Federalist party liked or did not like. Soon he began to side more often with the Republican party than the Federalist party. As a result, he lost his office after only one term.

President Madison sent Adams to Europe in 1814, where he helped write the peace treaty that ended the War of 1812. When James Monroe became president in 1817, he appointed Adams to secretary of state, where he excelled. Adams was a short, plump man that did not have many friends. However, he made the best possible bargains for his country. He helped settle a quarrel between the U.S. and England over the Oregon territory. He wrote the treaty in which the U.S. won Florida from Spain. He also played a significant role in the Monroe Doctrine.

In the presidential election of 1824, there were four primary candidates. In the electoral college, Andrew Jackson got the most votes, and Adams came in second. However, there wasn't a majority, which meant the final choice had to be made in the House of Representatives. Adams was chosen as the 6th President of the United States. He was the first son of a former president to be elected.

When Adams first took office, his friends gave him the advice to fire all of Monroe's appointees and name his own people to office. His advisers were concerned because many of the holdovers from Monroe's administration had supported Andrew Jackson in the presidential election. Now that Jackson had lost the race, his supporters were angry, and they believed Adams had made a corrupt bargain with Henry Clay to steal the election. They wanted revenge, so they made plans to block Adams at every turn until Jackson could be elected president in 1828. The advice was good, but he refused to take it because he didn't think it would be fair to reward his friends with political positions. The

Adams administration remained filled with people who did not wish the new president well.

John Quincy Adams was the first president to be photographed. He also became the first president to champion the government's role in making improvements for the benefit of trade. Both Monroe and Madison had vetoed government-funded road and canal construction projects because they believed them to be unconstitutional. Adams wanted the government to take an active role in expanding commerce. He was a strong supporter of the American System, which was built by Secretary of State Henry Clay. The American System meant to create a self-sufficient national economy. Clay believed that boosting a factory base in the North would help create important new markets for cotton grown in the South as well as grain and beef, which was raised in the West. In exchange, people in the South and West would buy goods that were manufactured in the North. In order to accomplish this, Clay proposed high tariffs on imported goods, funding for internal improvements, and strengthening of the national bank. This would help protect New England's growing factory economy, which was barely a decade old and keep it from having to compete with cheap European goods. New roads and canals would mean that farmers would be able to bring their crops to market more efficiently. Also, a stronger national bank would produce the sort of stable national credit system necessary for internal trade to boom.

Many opposed the American system for two reasons: one is that they were merely trying to make Adams look bad so that Jackson would win the election in 1828. The other was that many were worried that the federal government was becoming too powerful. Because of the opposition that Adams faced within Congress, he was able to win passage of only two public works bills. The first extended the Cumberland Road into Ohio, and the seconded funded the construction of a new canal between the Ohio River and the Chesapeake Bay.

Adam's four years as president were probably the most unhappy years of his life. Many people admired his intelligence, but almost no one liked him. His sharp tongue made him many enemies. In the election of 1828, Adams was defeated by Andrew Jackson, just as his advisors had warned him when he first took office. Adams was deeply hurt by his loss, and he went back to his home in Massachusetts. In 1830, the sixty-three-year-old Adams ran for a seat in the House of Representatives and won. He became the first president to serve in Congress after leaving the White House. Some said he would be disgraced by serving in Congress after being president to which Adams replied by saying that no man was disgraced by serving his country.

For the next seventeen years, Adams served in Congress. He fought for the things he had always believed in. He also helped establish the Smithsonian Institution. He fought against slavery and for civil rights as well as free speech. He was one of the nation's finest Congressmen. He was at his desk on February 21, 1848, when he fell unconscious. Two days later, he passed away.

ANDREW JACKSON
7TH PRESIDENT: 1829-1837

Andrew Jackson was the first president born in a log cabin of a poor family. His father and mother had come from Ireland only two years before his birth. His father died before he was born, and his mother died when he was only fourteen. He marked a new era in American politics because he was the first common man ever elected. When he was nine years old, he read the Declaration of Independence aloud for a group of men who could not read for themselves. These men formed a Revolutionary Army unit, and Jackson watched them at work. He did not want to sit on the sidelines, so he made himself useful since he was an excellent horseman. He carried messages from one unit to another. A year later, he was captured by the British. While captive, he was hit across the head when he refused to clean an English officer's boots. The blow left a scar on his face, but it left more than just a physical scar, it left a deep hatred for the English.

After the war, Jackson studied law and then moved to a frontier village called Nashville in what is now Tennessee. Tall, handsome, and popular, Jackson liked life on the frontier. He was a gambler, hot-tempered, and reckless. He was wounded twice in duels and once killed a man who he thought had insulted his wife.

When the people in Tennessee raised an army to fight the Creek Indians, Jackson was elected general. He had no military training, but he proved to be an excellent general and went on to defeat the Creek Indians. The next year, 1814, he was made a general in the federal army. In the last battle of the War of 1812, he defeated the British at New Orleans and became a national hero. Jackson got his nickname "Old Hickory" after a soldier who served with him during the War of 1812 said he was "tough as a hickory."

At the time, Florida still belonged to Spain. Seminole Indians living in Florida sometimes made raids across the Georgia border, so President Monroe sent

Jackson with a small army to stop these raids. The hot-headed Jackson said the Spanish were protecting the Seminoles and that Florida really ought to belong to the U.S. Jackson not only chased the Seminoles into Florida, but he also attacked and captured the Spanish city of Pensacola. This could very well have led to war with Spain; however, Secretary of State John Quincy Adams managed to keep the peace.

In 1824, the people of Tennessee nominated Jackson for president. It may be that Jackson did not really want to be elected, as he had already been elected to Congress three different times. Each time he had quit before his term ended. He was quoted as saying, "Do you think that I am such a darned fool as to think myself fit for the presidency? No sir...I can command a body of men in a rough way, but I am not fit to be president."

In the election, Jackson was defeated by John Quincy Adams. Jackson's friends told him he had been cheated, which was not true. However, Jackson believed his friends, and from that day, he set out to defeat Adams as he might have set out to win a battle.

During this time, people from all over the United States were moving west. New states were coming into the Union, and new frontiers were being born. The old rule that only men who owned property could vote was being changed. Since Jackson was himself a frontiersman, to the people moving west, looking for new land and a new life, he was a hero. In the election of 1828, Jackson was overwhelmingly swept into office.

Jackson believed that ordinary Americans, such as farmers and pioneers, had enough sense to make political decisions for themselves. This idea was the cornerstone of his democracy, and the people loved him for it. Because of his frequent direct appeals to the public for support, Jackson is widely considered to have been the first 'modern' president. He believed that the president spoke with the voice of the people because the president was the only government official elected by all Americans.

From all over the country, the common people who admired Jackson came to hear him take the oath of office. A mob of twenty thousand supporters followed Jackson's carriage from the Capitol to the White House. Many followed Jackson into the White House itself, through the windows as well as the doors. They broke the fine china, spit tobacco juice on the carpets, and stood on chairs to get a better view. Jackson was unable to maintain order, so he fled the building through a rear window and escaped to a nearby hotel. Eventually, waiters drew the unruly crowd outside by placing tubs of punch on the front lawn. The damage was expensive, but Jackson did not mind because the people were happy for his victory.

When Andrew Jackson wed Rachel Donelson in 1791, she was technically still married to her first husband. However, both Donelson and Jackson had believed at the time that a divorce had been granted. The divorce wasn't actually finalized until 1793. A few months later, they were married again, this time legally. This mistake haunted them during the 1828 presidential campaign. The National Republicans accused Jackson of adultery because he and Rachel had lived together before being legally married. Jackson tried to shield his wife from the attacks, but Rachel eventually learned of the smear campaign in the press. She quickly fell ill and died less than two months after the election. She was buried in the dress that she had bought to wear at her husband's inauguration.

The most important legislation of Jackson's first term in office was the Indian Removal Act of 1830. For years, the state of Georgia had been trying to confiscate and sell land belonging to the Cherokees. They were among the Five Civilized Tribes that had adopted the ways of American society in order to live peacefully. To become acceptable to the settlers, the Cherokees had taken up European-style farming techniques, developed a written language, and adopted their own constitution. But neither the government of Georgia or President Jackson had any respect for them.

Jackson was well known for his dislike of Native Americans. The Indian Removal Act gave him the power to remove them from the South and force them to relocate to unsettled lands west of the Mississippi. Over the next few years, Jackson used federal troops to force the Cherokees, Choctaws, Creeks, Chickasaws, and Seminoles to abandon one hundred million acres of land. The Cherokees asked the Supreme Court for help and argued that their tribe was legally a foreign nation and thus not subject to the removal law. Chief Justice John Marshall denied their petition but did point out that only the federal government had sovereignty over their tribe. Therefore, the state laws of Georgia did not apply to them, and no Americans could settle their land without Cherokee permission. Even so, Georgia ignored the decision and Jackson refused to enforce it, so the forced removal of the Cherokees continued.

During his last year in office, Jackson's attention turned west to Texas, which was still Mexican territory. While he longed to add Texas to the Union, he also felt bound to honor Mexico's sovereignty. He was worried that the admission of Texas as a slave state would disturb the balance between the North and the South.

In December of 1835, settlers in Texas revolted against the new Mexican government lead by Antonio Lopez de Santa Anna, mainly because Santa Anna had outlawed slavery. Raising an army, Santa Anna led Mexican troops into Texas to put down the rebellion. After a thirteen day siege Santa Anna's army defeated the small group of Texans at the Battle of the Alamo.

Santa Anna's victory there was short-lived, and six weeks later an army of Texans under the command of Sam Houston won both the battle of San Jacinto and independence for Texas. The Texans' battle cry was, "Remember the Alamo!" On July 4, Congress agreed to recognize the new Republic of Texas, which was the first step in making Texas a part of the Union.

One of Jackson's final actions before leaving office was to issue the Specie Circular. This presidential order declared that paper money could no longer be used to purchase federal land. Instead, buyers would have to use gold or silver coins. Such a drastic reversal of policy sent land prices tumbling, and the collapse in the land market led to a series of bankruptcies. By the time Jackson left office, businesses all over the country were closing, and with the government still refusing to accept paper money, the panic spread.

MARTIN VAN BUREN
8TH PRESIDENT: 1837 - 1841

Martin Van Buren did not grow up wealthy. His father was a poor farmer and tavern keeper in Kinderhook, New York, which is where Martin was born and raised. The Van Burens spoke Dutch at home, and he was raised according to European customs. After school, Van Buren often helped his father in the tavern, where famous politicians such as Alexander Hamilton and Aaron Burr would stop in on their way to and from the state capital Albany, NY. Young Martin loved to listen to their arguments, and he developed an interest in politics that would drive him the rest of his life. Van Buren went to school for only a few years. When he was fourteen he got a job in a lawyer's office, and at twenty-one, he became a lawyer himself. He was also interested in politics and held several state offices. He used these offices to give jobs to people who would vote for him and for his political acquaintances. By doing this, he built up quite a following, and in 1821 he was elected to the U.S. Senate.

During this time, Andrew Jackson was running for president. Van Buren was a brilliant politician, but he did not inspire loyalty like Jackson. Van Buren knew this and realized his own political future depended on Jackson, so he worked to help Jackson win his election. When Jackson was elected president, he appointed Van Buren secretary of state.

Van Buren was a good secretary of state, but many other men in Jackson's cabinet were more well known. No one suspected that Van Buren would ever become president. In time, Van Buren made a point to get to know Jackson on a personal level. Even though Van Buren disliked horseback riding, he rode with Jackson quite often to stay in his good graces. When Jackson ran for a second term, he asked that Van Buren be made vice president. It was largely because of Jackson's help that Van Buren was elected as the 8th President of the United States in 1836.

In 1837, the year Martin Van Buren became president following the election of 1836, Washington was still a swampy, malaria-ridden town. Open sewers wound through unpaved streets, while pigs and chickens wandered about. In marketplaces, slaves were bought and sold.

At his inauguration, Van Buren spoke directly about the issue of slavery, which he had avoided during the campaign. He said that he would fight any attempts to abolish slavery in the South because southern states had the right to decide the matter for themselves. What Van Buren wanted was for the issue to go away, but that would not happen. He was forced to confront slavery again when Texas applied for admission to the Union shortly after winning its independence from Mexico.

If Texas were to be admitted, it would most assuredly have to be as a slave state because it was Mexico's attempt to abolish slavery in Texas that had started the rebellion in the first place. Admitting Texas as a slave state would upset the delicate balance of power between free and slave states that had been preserved by the Missouri Compromise. Despite Van Buren's strong support for slavery, he decided to oppose the admission of Texas because he feared the political consequences. He worried that admitting Texas as a slave state would reopen the entire debate. The President's decision was unpopular in the South and it was attacked by many who wanted to expand the territory of the country.

During the last few months in office, Andrew Jackson had issued the Specie Circular, an executive order intended to curb inflation and control land speculation in the West. It stated that paper money could no longer be used to purchase government land, and instead, buyers would have to pay for the land with specie (gold or silver).

During the nineteenth century, paper money was valuable only if it was backed by, or could be exchanged for, precious metals such as gold and silver. Coins made from these metals were known as specie. Under this banking system, a one-dollar bill could be exchanged at any time for a dollar's worth of specie.

The Specie Circular forced buyers of land to exchange their paper money for gold or silver, but this created a demand for specie that the banks couldn't meet. Because of the inflation and bad loans the banks had, there was no longer enough gold and silver to back all the paper money in circulation, which in turn made the value of paper money fall.

The Panic of 1837 began when several banks in New York City stopped converting paper money into gold and silver. Loans became harder to come by, and as a result, speculators who were denied credit stopped buying land; so, land prices fell sharply. Nearly one thousand banks around the country failed, and when they did, work on the internal development projects that the banks had been financing also stopped. This put many people out of work. In some cities, hungry people were rioting for food.

Van Buren had a plan to set up an independent treasury, run by the government, which could protect federal money from irresponsible loans. Several congressmen opposed this plan because they didn't want government funds taken from the banks in their home states. It wasn't until 1840, which was the last year of Van Buren's term, that Congress finally passed the Independent Treasury Act.

Van Buren tried his best to be a good president, but the economy was in a downturn, and he was an easy target for blame. Van Buren was a small, dapper, and refined man, and he was often criticized for the way that he appeared in public. He wore a coat with a velvet collar and tight-fitting gloves made from very soft leather. He traveled through the muddy and smelly streets of Washington in a luxurious green coach driven by men in elaborate uniforms. As a result, people often complained that the president behaved more like a king than a Democrat. What made matters worse was that he was a snappy dresser, and he liked to eat well so his enemies would tell stories of how he would drink foreign wines and use gold forks and silver plates. This was the same kind of gossip that Van Buren had once spread to help Andrew Jackson defeat John Quincy Adams. Now it was enough to make hungry people without jobs vote against Van Buren. He only served for one term as president.

Back in New York, the former president remained active in local and national politics, speaking out against slavery. He died at home in Kinderhook at the age of 79.

WILLIAM HENRY HARRISON
9TH PRESIDENT: 1841

William Henry Harrison was born on a large Virginia plantation just before the outbreak of the American Revolution. His father, Benjamin Harrison, signed the Declaration of Independence. When William Henry Harrison was fourteen, he went to Hampden-Sidney College. He studied the Greek and Latin classics and enjoyed reading. Later, he studied medicine because his father wanted him to. When his father died, Harrison quit school and joined the army. For several years he served on the northwest frontier and fought against the Native Americans.

Harrison was only twenty-seven when he was appointed governor of the Indiana territory. He served in this office for twelve years.

During this time, relations between Native Americans and the American settlers were on the decline. American settlers had been pushing the Native Americans out of the Ohio River Valley. Thomas Jefferson had wanted to integrate the native people into society by teaching them how to farm in the European fashion and how to trade and sell. Unfortunately, neither the American settlers or the Native Americans had any interest in Jefferson's plan. Instead, the American settlers kept taking Native American land, either by force or by deception. By 1810, settlers had seized one hundred million acres of fertile land that once belonged to the natives.

When the famous Shawnee chief Tecumseh saw what was happening, he tried to put an end to the land grabs. Tecumseh took a stand against further American expansion into the West. The Native Americans resented being forced off their traditional hunting grounds with the promise that it would never happen again. Tecumseh wanted to form an alliance with all the frontier tribes from the Canadian border down to Florida. Tecumseh understood that American settlers were using alcohol to cheat Native Americans out of their land.

On November 7, 1811, while Tecumseh was away in the south trying to recruit allies, Harrison arrived near Prophetstown and arranged to meet with the town's spiritual leader, Tenskwatawa, the following day. Tenskwatawa was not a military leader but attacked Harrison's army the next morning. In the ensuing Battle of Tippecanoe Creek, General William Henry Harrison, who would later become president, was taken by surprise as the warriors from Prophetstown attacked his army. Harrison and his men stood their ground for more than two hours and after the battle and burned Prophetstown to the ground destroying the winter food supplies. General Harrison led one thousand soldiers in that battle, which made him quite famous. He was given the nickname Old Tippecanoe. Tecumseh vowed revenge and fought alongside the British in Canada during the War of 1812, where he was killed.

During the War of 1812, Harrison served as a general in the American army. He briefly served in Congress but then left to live on his farm in North Bend, Ohio, where he thought he had left public life forever. However, people still remembered Old Tippecanoe.

In 1840, Martin Van Buren ran for a second term. The Whigs nominated Harrison to run against him. Although he had never taken a very large part in politics, he was still popular due to his military career. The Whigs needed a popular hero, not a politician. They did not even say what Harrison or the Whig party believed in; they just ran against Van Buren's record and unpopularity as president.

Since the country was in the middle of a very bad depression, the people were looking for a change. American heroes were frontiersmen and fighters, which is precisely what Van Buren was to them. In 1840, William Henry Harrison became the 9th President of the United States.

As soon as Harrison took office, long lines of people were asking him for jobs. He wanted to help, and he tried, but he was worn out by his campaign and his inauguration speech, which was the longest in history at one hour and forty-five minutes. Harrison caught a cold which turned into pneumonia and Harrison died one month after his inauguration. He is remembered for having the shortest term of all the presidents as well as being the first president to die in office.

JOHN TYLER

10TH PRESIDENT: 1841 - 1845

John Tyler's father was the governor of Virginia and a friend of Thomas Jefferson. He grew up believing in the state's rights and that the powers of the federal government should be limited. When he was seventeen, he graduated from William and Mary. Then at twenty-one, he was elected to the Virginia legislature. From there, he served in the House of Representatives, as governor of Virginia and in the U.S. Senate.

The Whig party nominated Tyler for vice president mainly due to him being from the South. William Henry Harrison was from the West, so the Whigs wanted a vice president who could help get more southern votes. Tyler was a good-looking, soft-spoken man that was well-liked in his home state of Virginia.

His record in Congress showed clearly what he believed in, which was that the federal government should keep out of the state's business. He had always voted against spending federal money on things like roads and harbors. Initially, he had been a Democrat, not a Whig, and supported Andrew Jackson for President. But soon, Tyler thought Jackson took advantage of his power, and Tyler turned against him. Because of this, Tyler was viewed as a Whig even though his voting record indicated otherwise. He still believed strongly in state's rights.

William Henry Harrison was the first president to die in office, and his death caused a great deal of confusion. Vice President John Tyler's transition to power should have been simple, but it was anything but that. Tyler was not even aware the president was sick. He was surprised when a government clerk woke him at his home in Virginia with the news that Harrison was dead.

Tyler's problem was that he had been nominated as vice president to balance the Whig ticket. Now that he was in control and did not accept the Whig's nationalist policies, the party leaders did not trust him. Especially the most important Whig leader, Henry Clay.

During the single month that William Henry Harrison was President, it seemed that Henry Clay was actually running the government and was for a strong federal government. On important matters, Harrison let Clay decide what needed to be done, which was precisely what Clay had hoped for. Tyler, on the other hand, believed that a strong, federal government threatened individual freedoms.

Clay and his followers tried to limit Tyler's power by refusing to recognize him at the new president. They referred to him as "the acting president." Tyler did not let this sway his thinking or actions. He made the point by returning unopened mail addressed to "Acting President Tyler."

Tyler clashed with Clay time and again, and the conflict came to a head over the topic of a national bank. Clay had wanted to bring back a national bank ever since Jackson's undoing of the Second Bank of the United States. He pushed bills through Congress chartering a Third Bank two times, and both times Tyler angered the Whigs by vetoing them. To protest Tyler's vetoes, the entire cabinet resigned. Tyler quickly appointed a new cabinet, which agreed with his policies, but he lost all support from the Whigs.

Tyler still had a great deal of power when it came to foreign affairs, which he put to use. He resolved a border dispute with Canada, which granted the United States slightly more than half of the disputed land along the Maine border. The Webster-Ashburton Treaty fixed the U.S. - Canadian border all the way from the Atlantic Ocean west to the Rocky Mountains.

Down south, Tyler began to address the matter of Texan statehood, which had been in limbo since the Van Buren administration. By 1843, most Texans had grown tired of waiting, and their representatives had begun talking with Great Britain about the possibility of remaining independent under British protection. Around this time, Tyler began his own secret talks with Texas, which led to a treaty that was rejected by the Senate in 1844. This treaty was written by Tyler's new Secretary of State John C. Calhoun and included a section that glorified slavery, which is why it was voted down.

Tyler was in his fifties but looked much younger. Shortly after he took office, his wife died. He married again to a woman named Julia Gardiner, who was thirty years younger. Tyler was the first president to be married while in office.

In the election of 1844, Tyler was eager to be reelected because he wanted to ensure Texas joined the Union. But neither the Whigs nor the Democrats wanted him, and when he tried to form a third party, it failed. Since Tyler was no longer a member of the Whig party, they chose Henry Clay, who had previously run for president in 1824 and 1832. The Democrats decided to go another route as well. They nominated James K. Polk, who ran on the platform of expanding the U.S. Polk's victory, persuaded Congress that the public wanted Texas to become part of the Union. As Tyler's final act as president, before he left office, he signed a joint resolution of Congress admitting Texas to the Union.

When his term was over, he went back to Virginia. Later as the Civil War was beginning, he was elected to the Confederate Congress. He died before that Congress ever met.

JAMES K. POLK
11TH PRESIDENT: 1845 - 1849

James Polk was the oldest of ten children. He was born in North Carolina, but he and his family moved to Tennessee when he was eleven years old. It was still frontier country at the time and his family prospered there, eventually owning thousands of acres worked by more than fifty slaves. Polk's father was a farmer, but the Polk was too sickly to do much to help his father. He was troubled by stones in his gallbladder. When he was seventeen, Polk underwent a dangerous and painful operation to remove the stones. The surgeon gave him only liquor to ease the pain. He spent most of his time reading and went on to graduate with top honors at the University of North Carolina where he studied law. He was elected to the U.S. House of Representatives, and from 1835 to 1839, he was the speaker of the House. He was a big fan of Andrew Jackson and worked hard to pass the laws Jackson wanted.

Polk left Congress to run for governor of Tennessee, where he was elected. He was defeated for reelection twice. It might have seemed that his career was over, but Polk had a determined spirit that wouldn't let him quit.

During the 1840s, Americans were eager to expand the territory of the United States. Ahh the time Polk was an unknown candidate but proved the strength of this cause by defeating Henry Clay in the presidential election of 1844 and became the 11th President of the United States. Polk quickly focused his attention on fulfilling the nation's "manifest destiny," which was a popular belief that it was proper and inevitable for the U.S. government to control all of North America.

Most people believed that the United States was carrying out a mission to create an "empire for liberty" from the Atlantic to the Pacific. Polk often used the idea to justify his actions, especially when taking new territory.

Because the annexation of Texas had already been completed during the last days of Tyler's term, Polk turned his attention to the acquisition of Oregon. Both the U.S. and Great Britain had longtime claims to the Oregon Territory. At first, Polk refused to negotiate with the British. Eventually, Polk agreed to a compromise, and a new boundary was set at the Forty-ninth parallel, granting to the U.S. the present-day states of Oregon and Washington. Polk became the first president to govern the United States that extended all the way from the Atlantic Ocean to the Pacific. After settling this dispute, he turned his sights towards the Mexican colonies in the Southwest and California. Soon he would become the first president to act militarily in support of the cause of manifest destiny.

Even after Texas formally joined the Union in 1845, the U.S. and Mexico continued to fight over Texas's southern border. Congress insisted that it be the Rio Grande, while the Mexicans refused to recognize any border south of the Nueces River. Polk tried bargaining and offered to pay Mexico for the disputed land. When the Mexicans refused, Polk sent troops under General Zachary Taylor to the Rio Grande.

In 1846, Mexican troops engaged U.S. soldiers. Eight days later, Polk asked Congress for a declaration of war because Mexican soldiers had "shed American blood upon American soil." Congress agreed and approved his request.

The Mexican War became the central political event during Polk's presidency. His party rallied to him, while the Whigs became divided. Those from the south and west approved of the war, while those in the north believed that the Mexican War was part of a secret plan to expand slavery into the southwest.

The Mexican army greatly outnumbered U.S. forces in the area, but superior American technology and strategy helped the U.S. prevail. This, in part, was due to the revolver, which was invented by Samuel Colt, which was very powerful in combat. The success of his revolver during the Mexican War led to a large government contract. Colt used the money to build the world's largest private armory, where he made significant advances in the use of interchangeable parts.

The Mexican War ended in 1848 with the signing of the Treaty of Guadalupe Hidalgo. The treaty stated that Mexico ceded to the United States more than five hundred thousand square miles of territory, in what is now all of California, and Nevada and part of Utah, Arizona, and New Mexico. In return, the U.S. paid Mexico fifteen million dollars. It agreed to allow Mexicans already living on the land to remain there if they so choose. The Mexican Cession was the nation's largest acquisition of land since the Louisiana Purchase.

During the 1844 campaign, Polk had promised that if he won, he would not run for reelection. Even though he was now extremely popular and would have easily won, he kept his word and announced he would retire in 1849. Although Polk expected to enjoy a long and peaceful retirement at his home in Nashville, he fell ill during a goodwill tour of the South shortly after leaving office. His condition grew worse, and he died shortly thereafter.

ZACHARY TAYLOR

12TH PRESIDENT: 1849 - 1850

Zachary Taylor was raised in a small frontier village called Louisville, Kentucky. His father was an officer in the Revolutionary War. He was raised romanticizing about the battle. When he was twenty-two, Taylor joined the army as a private. Two years later, he was made lieutenant. He fought in Native American campaigns and in the War of 1812. He then fought against Chief Black Hawk and against the Seminoles in Florida. During the Seminole War, Taylor became a general.

Texas became part of the Union in 1845, and that is when there was a heated debate of where the southern border of Texas was, which led to the Mexican War. In the Battle of Buena Vista, General

Taylor defeated a Mexican army that was four times as large has his. This turned him into a national hero.

The Whig party wanted a hero for its presidential candidate in 1848. There were two options, General Taylor and General Winfield Scott. Both were soldiers, but that is all they had in common. Scott dressed in handsome uniforms, and his boots were always polished. His soldiers nicknamed him 'Old Fuss and Feathers.' Taylor wore the same dirty clothes he wore on his farm, and his soldiers called him 'Old Rough and Ready.'

At the time, presidential candidates never attended party conventions. They stayed at home and awaited the results. To notify Taylor of his nomination, the president of the Whig convention sent the general a letter, but he didn't put any postage on the envelope. Sending mail without postage was common at the time because it forced the recipient to pay the postage that was due. Taylor received so many postage-due letters from admirers that he told the post office to stop delivering them, as he did not want to have to pay for them all. Because of this, he never received his notice that he was nominated.

Weeks later, the Whigs realized what had happened, and they sent another letter, this time with the postage already paid.

In the young, fierce frontier nation of 1848, Old Fuss and Feathers did not stand a chance against Old Rough and Ready, and so Taylor was elected as the 12th President of the United States. It could be argued that no man ever became president that knew less about what he was supposed to do. He was simply a soldier, used to giving and taking orders with little knowledge of politics.

The most important issue facing Zachary Taylor when he took office was the possible extension of slavery into the territories of the Mexican Cession. The North and South both held opposing views on what should be done. Taylor had been careful not to reveal his opinion on the issue during the campaign. He let people assume that since he owned slaves that he must support slavery. They were shocked to learn after the election that the new president intended to oppose the extension of slavery into the new territories.

Taylor proposed to Congress that two-thirds of the Mexican Cession be set aside for huge new states in

New Mexico and California, and both of these states be free. Southerners were furious at this plan, and people in South Carolina even threatened to secede from the Union.

When gold was found outside Sacramento, statehood for California became a pressing matter. As a result of the Gold Rush, the population of California grew from ten thousand to one hundred thousand in just a few years. It quickly became one of the wealthiest territories in the nation. A compromise was called for in order to try and avoid a civil war. Senator Henry Clay proposed a series of resolutions designed to satisfy both sides. His plan was later called the Great Compromise, and it called for the admission of California as a free state, leaving the issue of slavery in the rest of the Mexican Cession up to the people who lived there. Most northerners were willing to accept this, but southerners needed a little more convincing if they were going to agree.

In order to appease them, Clay offered them the Fugitive Slave Act. This bill made northerners responsible for returning runaway slaves to their southern masters. Before this, escaped slaves were allowed to remain free if they could successfully reach the North. President Taylor opposed this and planned to veto any bill that made possible the spread of slavery. However, on the Fourth of July, 1850, he became ill, and five days later, he died.

MILLARD FILLMORE

13TH PRESIDENT: 1850 - 1853

Millard Fillmore's father had a small farm in the Finger Lakes of New York. Young Fillmore worked there until he was fifteen. He attended a one-room school whenever he could, which was not often. At eighteen, he was out of place at the school with the other seven and eight-year-old boys also in attendance. The teacher was a pretty red-haired girl named Abigail Powers, who taught him well. When he was twenty, he moved to Buffalo, New York, and got a job as a teacher. At the same time, he was studying law. After some time, he was admitted to the bar and eventually married Abigail.

He quickly became a success, and in 1832 he was elected to Congress as a member of the Whig party.

In Congress, he voted against admitting Texas to the Union, because it permitted slavery. In 1848, the Whig party nominated Zachary Taylor for president and Fillmore for vice president. Although Fillmore had a reputation for being a dull speaker and mediocre leader, he was also known as an honorable man. He never smoked or drank. During the 1848 election campaign, Fillmore was largely ignored. He didn't even meet Zachary Taylor until after the election. He was excluded from any role in shaping the new cabinet.

While vice president, Fillmore presided over one of the most important debates in American history involving whether the new western territories would be free states or slave states. Both the Democrats and the Whigs were split on the matter. Senator Henry Clay from Kentucky offered a compromise, which later became known as the Compromise of 1850. Its main point was that California would come into the Union as a free state. In return, there would be a law called the Fugitive Slave Act, where an owner could follow his runaway slave into a free state and recapture him.

After Zachary Taylor's death, Millard Fillmore became the thirteenth President of the United

States. As president, Fillmore was in favor of the compromise as he thought it was the only way the nation could avoid a civil war. In September of 1850, Fillmore signed the five separate bills that made up the Great Compromise, including the Fugitive Slave Act. Many northerners hated this law. Abolitionist newspapers often wrote about cases in which free blacks were enslaved by mistake or taken by dishonest slave catchers.

Antislavery activists tried to obstruct the law whenever possible. Some of them offered free legal advice to escaped slaves, and others posted notices warning blacks of the dangers posed by kidnappers. Fillmore knew all of this but still thought supporting the compromise was the only way to prevent secession. He also believed that if he were able to resolve the crisis, he might even be reelected.

Because he signed the law, many Whigs in the North turned against him, and as a result, he was not nominated by the Whig party for reelection. And before long, the whole party began to fall apart. Fillmore was the last Whig president.

As president, Fillmore did do one thing of lasting importance. For two hundred years, Japan had refused to trade or to have anything to do with other countries. In 1853 Fillmore sent Commodore Matthew Perry to visit Japan. Perry met with the Japanese emperor, who agreed to let American trading ships visit Japan. This became known as the "opening" of Japan.

FRANKLIN PIERCE

14TH PRESIDENT: 1853 - 1857

Franklin Pierce came from a well-known New England family where his father was governor of New Hampshire. As a boy, he loved listening to the stories of battle told by his older brothers, who were serving in the army during the War of 1812. These stories eventually inspired him to become a soldier himself.

Franklin was elected to the state legislature, and he later was elected to the U.S. House of Representatives and then to the United States Senate. He was the youngest member of the Senate. As a young Congressman, Pierce had married the pretty daughter of the president of Bowdoin College. When the Mexican War started, Pierce enlisted as a private. President Polk promptly made him a colonel, then a general, even without much experience.

In 1852 a convention met in Baltimore to name the Democratic party's candidate for President. At this time, Pierce was little known outside his home state. Everybody thought the candidate would be one of the leaders of the party, but none of the well-known men could get enough votes to win. Finally, on the forty-ninth ballot, Pierce was named as a compromise. Franklin Peirce went on to win the election and become the 14th President of the United States.

Peirce was famous throughout New Hampshire as a brilliant courtroom lawyer, and people would come from all over to hear his courtroom speeches. He was such an accomplished speaker that he was able to deliver his entire inaugural address from memory. In the address, Pierce stated his personal belief that owning slaves was a legal right guaranteed by the Constitution; however, he also acknowledged that extremism on both sides was now threatening the Union.

During his term, the U.S. continued to expand. In 1853 his cabinet negotiated the ten-million-dollar purchase of territory in present-day Arizona and New Mexico, which totaled twenty-nine-thousand square miles. This was prime real estate because it lay along the path of a proposed transcontinental railroad. Cartographers could for the first time draw U.S. maps that showed the modern outline of the forty-eight continental states.

While the government was considering how to build the first transcontinental railroad, a senator from Illinois named Stephen Douglas was working to ensure that this took a northern route through his home state. He knew that wherever the railroad went, business opportunities would follow. Southerners also wanted the railroad to pass through their region, so Douglas decided to make a deal. If any railroad were going to be built across the Great Plains, a first step would have to be the organization of territories in Kansas and Nebraska. To encourage southerners to go along with his plan, Douglas included in his Kansas-Nebraska bill a provision that allowed the residents of those territories to decide for themselves whether or not to permit slavery.

This plan was controversial because it repealed the Missouri Compromise of 1820, which had outlawed slavery in all Louisiana Purchase lands, which included Kansas and Nebraska. It was clear that

Nebraskans would vote to prohibit slavery in their territory. Still, it was anybody's guess what Kansas would vote since they bordered on proslavery, Missouri. A hard and bloody fight was eminent.

Pierce backed the Kansas-Nebraska Act and passed it into law, but it caused more trouble than it solved. Abolitionists from New England poured into Kansas, hoping to win control of the territorial government. At the same time, gangs of proslavery supporters from Missouri organized to challenge them. During March of 1855, about four thousand Missourians crossed the border into Kansas and voted illegally. Some forced their way into the polls at gunpoint, and their votes helped elect a proslavery legislature.

Feeling that they had been cheated, some antislavery settlers responded with violence of their own, and civil war broke out in Kansas. Soon, more than two hundred people died there, which gave it the term 'Bleeding Kansas.' The violence was not limited to Kansas. Charles Sumner of Massachusetts was attacked on the floor of the U.S. Senate by representative Preston Brooks of South Carolina due to a heated debate over slavery. Brooks beat Sumner over the head with a cane.

By the end of Franklin Pierce's first term, the nation was hurtling toward its most terrible tragedy, the Civil War. A new anti-slavery party called the Republican party was formed. By the time the 1856 election came around, the country had lost whatever respect it once had for Pierce. The public response to his handling of the violence in Kansas made it obvious he couldn't win reelection, and Pierce himself did not want to remain in office any longer. Pierce went back home to New Hampshire, but even there, he was no longer popular.

JAMES BUCHANAN
15TH PRESIDENT: 1857-1861

James Buchanan was born in a log cabin a few miles outside Mercersburg, Pennsylvania. When he was five, his family moved into the town of Mercersburg, where his Irish immigrant father made a living as a merchant and farmer. Young Buchanan learned to add and subtract and keep books by clerking in his father's store. Later he studied law and went into politics. He was over six feet tall and broad-shouldered. When he was twenty-three years old, he was elected to the state legislature. At thirty, he was elected to Congress. He belonged to the Federalist Party, but this party was slowly breaking up. Buchanan then became a Democrat.

President Polk appointed Buchanan, his secretary of state. He helped settle the problems of the Oregon Territory and the Mexican War. Buchanan believed the United States was out to get more and more territory. Once he wrote that the U.S. should try to buy Cuba from Spain and if Spain would not sell Cuba, then the U.S. should take it by force.

By the election of 1856, slavery had become the biggest problem facing the United States. Many people in the North wanted to end slavery altogether. Southern slaveowners wanted slavery made legal in all the territories.

The new Republican party was against slavery. The Democratic party did not want to take any firm stance on slavery one way or the other. They hoped this wouldn't anger anybody and would help them win votes in the North and the South. Nobody was sure where Buchanan stood on slavery, so the Democrats made him their candidate. It was a close election, but James Buchanan became the 15th President of the United States.

As Buchanan took office in 1857, the most crucial task facing him was the prevention of civil war. Everyone wondered what the Buchanan administration would do to resolve the issue of slavery, particularly concerning its expansion into the western territories. At his inauguration, he announced that the conflict over slavery had a clear and simple solution. He pointed out that few Americans disputed the constitutionality of slavery in the southern states, where it had always existed. If these states could legally permit slavery within their borders, how could the federal government deny new states the same privilege? Allowing new territories to decide the slavery issue for themselves was, therefore, the proper and most reasonable course of action.

Buchanan had only been in office for two days when the Supreme Court handed down a decision that pleased the slave owners in the South. It was called the Dred Scott case, which ruled that slaves, from a legal point of view, were property, not citizens. The court thus supported Buchanan's argument that ownership of slaves was a constitutional right that the government could neither limit nor deny.

Legally, the matter finally seemed settled, but in actuality, it was anything but. There was much opposition to the morality of the issue as people believed that slavery was wrong and should be outlawed everywhere.

The nation's attention returned to Bleeding Kansas, which was now seeking statehood. One of Buchanan's earliest actions had been to appoint Robert Walker from Mississippi as territorial governor there. A loyal southerner, Walker had then put all of his weight behind the proslavery forces. At a convention in 1857, delegates approved a proslavery constitution for Kansas. Buchanan backed it and urged Congress to admit Kansas as a slave state. Stephen Douglas led the Senate opposition, insisting that all people in Kansas be allowed to vote on the constitution before Congress accepted it. Kansas allowed its people to vote on the matter, and it was determined by a wide margin to reject the pro-slavery Constitution. Buchanan ordered Congress to have them vote again, and once again, the people voted against it. Finally, Kansas was admitted to the Union as a free state. By that time, the nation was on the brink of civil war.

During this time, Republican Abraham Lincoln decided to challenge Democrat Stephen Douglas in the 1858 Senate race in Illinois. This was covered by the national press, and the campaign featured seven eloquent debates between the two men. During the debates, Lincoln forced Douglas to admit that he believed a territory could outlaw slavery within its borders. This position contradicted the Dred Scott decision, which held that owning slaves was a constitutional right. While Douglas's answer helped him defeat Lincoln in Illinois, where slavery was not popular, it hurt Douglas in the South. Later, this loss of southern support made it almost impossible for him to win the Democratic nomination for President. Lincoln, however, performed so well in his debates that even though he lost the election, he became a very famous politician across the country.

Buchanan is the only president never to have married his entire life. When he was twenty-eight, he became engaged to Anne Coleman, whose father was one of the wealthiest men in Pennsylvania. They fought, and she broke off the engagement. Rumors had circulated that she had ended their relationship because she thought Buchanan was only after her money, while, in fact, Buchanan was doing quite well as a lawyer and was worth about three hundred thousand dollars. Buchanan never considered marriage again. During his term as president, his orphaned niece, Harriet Lane, served as the official White House hostess.

Events in Kansas made it evident that Americans on both sides were willing to shed blood for their beliefs. During the last frantic months of his failed presidency, Buchanan tried to remain friendly to the South as he struggled to preserve the Union. He was conflicted as he did not believe that any state had the right to secede, and at the same time, he did not believe the Union had the right to force a state to stay in the Union. The southern states, one after another, began to secede from the Union. He was hopeful that if he did nothing, the sates that had left the Union would decide to rejoin. And so, he did nothing, and the Civil War began.

ABRAHAM LINCOLN
16TH PRESIDENT: 1861 - 1865

Abraham Lincoln was born in a log cabin in Kentucky to a poor farmer who drifted from one place to another along the frontier. When Abe was eight years old, the family moved to Indiana, where he helped build their log cabin. It only had three walls, and on the open side, a fire had to be kept going day and night. Lincoln barely had a year of formal schooling. Unlike his father, he did learn to read and write. One of his favorite books was Parson Weem's biography of George Washington. In time, Lincoln's family moved from Indiana to Illinois. By now, Abe was six feet, four inches tall with black hair and a high-pitched voice. Even as a boy, he had a great talent for telling stories. He could make people laugh and they enjoyed being around him. People grew to trust and believe in him.

As a young man, Lincoln got a job on a flatboat going to New Orleans. Back in Illinois, he got a job in a country store. It eventually failed, and he got other odd jobs. He worked as a surveyor for a while before finally, a friend told him he aught to be a lawyer. It was easier to be a lawyer at that time than it is now, so Lincoln borrowed books and studied. He learned fast and eventually passed the bar. He went on to be one of the top trial lawyers in Illinois. He never lost his strong accent.

He was elected to the state legislature and eventually to Congress. While in Congress, he proposed one important law that said the government should buy all the slaves in the District of Columbia and set them free. The law did not pass, but it showed how Lincoln felt on the matter. He believed slavery was wrong but did not believe it could be abolished without payment to the slave owners. He did not win a second term in Congress, so he went back to Illinois to practice law. The slavery debate became more and more heated as more territories joined the Union. Lincoln was opposed to the spread of slavery, and he wanted to help the poor of any race. He knew what it was to be poor. He began to make speeches in favor of keeping the territories free.

In 1858, the Illinois Republican party asked Lincoln to run for the Senate against Stephen Douglas. Douglas was in favor of letting each new state decide for itself whether or not to have slaves. In a famous series of speeches, Lincoln and Douglas debated this question. Douglas won the election, but the debates made a name for Lincoln across the country. For that reason, the Republican party chose him to run for president two years later.

It was a bitter election. The Democratic party split in two, one part in the South, one in the North. A new third party tried to find some compromise. The election was held in the fall of 1860 and Lincoln won and became the 16th President of the United States. He took office in March of 1861.

As Lincoln prepared for his inauguration, events were already overtaking his administration. In the four months since his election, seven states had seceded from the Union to form the Confederate States of America. Before taking office, Lincoln said that there would be "no bloodshed unless it is forced upon the government." He also stated that he intended to retain control of all federal property in the South. He made it clear that his primary concern was the preservation of the Union, not the abolition of slavery.

On April 12, 1861, southern soldiers fired on the Union-held Fort Sumter in Charleston, South Carolina. This was the start of the War Between the States, which was later named the Civil War. He responded to the Confederate attack by ordering a naval blockade of all southern ports. The purpose was to halt the export of cotton, the South's most important cash crop. The blockade also prevented the agricultural South from importing manufactured goods such as guns and clothing. The start of the war caused four more undecided states to join the Confederacy.

Because they expected a speedy victory, most northerners backed Lincolns call for troops with enthusiasm. A waved of patriotism swept across the North. At first, blacks were excluded from the Union army, but as time passed and the war took turns for the worse, two hundred thousand blacks were allowed to join the fight. The Confederacy was no less successful in raising an army. Regional pride was especially strong in the South, and volunteers flocked to enlist. Fathers and sons went off to battle, while mothers and daughters took over family and business responsibilities. Women also raised money, recruited soldiers, and served as nurses, spies, and scouts. A few even dressed as men and became soldiers.

The first real battle was fought on the banks of a creek called Bull Run in northeastern Virginia, just outside Washington, D.C. Since the battlefield was so close to the capital, several members of Congress rode out in carriages to see the defeat of the Confederacy and the end of the rebellion. Many even brought picnic lunches. They were in for a surprise when Confederate General "Stonewall" Jackson broke the Union attack and sent the federals scurrying back to Washington. The battle of Bull Run taught the Union that victory would not come easily.

Later that summer, Robert E. Lee, who was given command of the Confederate army, won a second victory at Bull Run. Following up on that victory, Lee led his troops across the Potomac River into the Union state of Maryland. At the battle of Antietam, Lee fought to a standstill where more than twenty thousand soldiers were killed or wounded, making it the bloodiest battle in American history. Afterward, Lee retreated back across the Potomac River.

Antietam, which could only loosely be called a Union victory, gave Lincoln the opportunity he needed to announce the Emancipation Proclamation. This executive order freed all the slaves still in areas of rebellion but not those living in Union slave states, such as Maryland or in captured Southern territory. It also refocused the government from the preservation of the Union to the abolition of slavery.

Lincoln made George Meade commander of the Union army, and just three days after his promotion, he and General Lee met on the battlefield at Gettysburg. For the next seventy-two hours, their armies fought with one another as the outcome of the war hung in the balance. Lee lost more than twenty thousand men, or nearly a third of his army, at Gettysburg, while the Union lost nearly twenty-three thousand.

On November 19, 1863, Lincoln visited Gettysburg for the dedication of a battlefield cemetery at that location. The speech he gave became known as the Gettysburg Address and was just 272 words long. It didn't mention slavery, the battle, or even the Union army. It captured the reasons why the war was now being fought. After he finished, the crowd burst into applause.

In March of 1864, Lincoln turned over command of the Union troops to Ulysses S Grant. Grant had captured important Confederate forts in Tennessee and led Union troops to victory in Vicksburg, Mississippi. Meanwhile, Union General William Sherman captured Atlanta and began his famously destructive March to the Sea through Georgia. With no rebel army left that far south to offer any resistance, Sherman's March to the Sea undermined the South's ability to wage war by smashing railroads, factories, farms, and plantations.

In April of 1865, General Robert E. Lee surrendered to General Ulysses S. Grant. Five days later, President Lincoln and the First Lady went to see a play at a Washington theater. During the play, an actor named John Wilkes Booth stepped into the box behind Lincoln and shot him in the back of the head, and killed him.

ANDREW JOHNSON

17TH PRESIDENT: 1865 - 1869

Andrew Johnson's father worked as a handyman in a tavern in Raleigh, North Carolina. His mother was a maid in the same tavern. Johnson's father died when he was three years old, and his mother had to provide for the family by herself. He never attended school, and as a young boy, he apprenticed to a tailor. He did not enjoy this at all, and when he was sixteen, he ran away to the little town of Greenville, Tennessee, and went into business for himself as a tailor. He was successful, and when he turned eighteen, he married Eliza McCardle. She was only sixteen, but she had been to school. She taught her husband to write and helped him with his reading.

Johnson was a stocky young man with a hard mouth and no humor. He rarely laughed, but he had great drive to get ahead in the world. He would walk several miles back and forth to a school that let him take part in student debates. He had a big voice, a mind like a steel trap and tongue like a whip. Many of the students who were far better educated than he was were afraid to debate with him.

As soon as Johnson made a little money, he brought his mother and brothers and sisters to live with him. He always thought of himself as the champion of the poor and the weak against the rich and strong.

Most of the people who lived in Johnson's area of Tennessee were farmers or small businessmen. They elected him to the town council before he was twenty-one. He was only thirty-three when he was elected to Congress. At the age of forty-five, he became the governor of Tennessee. He went on to serve two terms and was elected to the U.S. Senate.

While Johnson's father had never owned much of anything, including slaves, Johnson believed that the right to own slaves was guaranteed by the Constitution. As a Democrat, while in the Senate, he voted with the South on almost every issue.

After Lincoln was elected, the southern states left the Union, Tennessee being included. As the states seceded, every Southerner left Congress, except for one, Andrew Johnson. He said, "I voted against Lincoln; I spoke against him. I spent my money to defeat him. But still, I love my country." Johnson became somewhat of a hero in the North. When Lincoln ran for a second term, the Republicans nominated Johnson for vice president. They never expected him to be president. Once Lincoln was murdered, Johnson became the 17th President of the United States.

Less than three hours after the president's death, the former tailor's apprentice was sworn into office. At the time, he had been vice president only forty-one days. Lincoln had won the Civil War for the Union. It was now up to Johnson to tackle the equally enormous task of reconstruction. He would have to reunite a nation in which neighbor had fought neighbor and brother had fought brother.

Johnson shared Lincoln's view that the country needed to forgive, forget, and welcome back the rebels. His plan was simple: under the direction of federal governors, the former Confederate states would draft new constitutions abolishing slavery and renouncing secession. After that, they would be free to govern themselves as before. Johnson also proposed that the citizenship of southerners be restored once they had taken a simple oath of allegiance.

This plan was not successful because Radical Republicans in Congress wanted to punish the South for seceding. These congressmen were worried about the Democratic party rising again in the southern states, and they still remembered how southern Democrats had dominated the federal government before Lincoln's election in 1860.

The southern economy was decimated by the Civil War and brought poverty to every level of southern society. The four million newly liberated slaves, now known as freedmen, were hit the hardest because they had started with the least. The Thirteenth Amendment abolished slavery and liberated all those slaves not already freed by the Emancipation Proclamation. The problem was the freedmen did not know what to do with their freedom. They owned little more than the clothes on their back. While Congress tried to help them with education programs, southerners did everything they could to keep the freedmen poor and powerless.

The Black Codes were a series of measures adopted by southern states to deny blacks their basic rights as citizens, such as the right to vote. Radical Republicans responded by passing the Civil Rights Act of 1866, which outlined the basic rights to which all Americans, regardless of skin color, were entitled to. Because he was a racist, Johnson vetoed the bill but the Republicans had enough votes in Congress to override this veto, and the bill became law despite the president's opposition.

Over time, blacks were able to achieve several political successes. In 1870, Hiram R. Revels of Mississippi became the first black elected to the Senate when he won the seat formerly occupied by Confederate president Jefferson Davis.

The conflict between Johnson and the Radical Republicans reached a crisis when the president fired Secretary of War Edwin Stanton. Like the rest of Johnson's cabinet, Stanton had been a holdover from the Lincoln administration. He was also a leader of the Radical Republicans and had been working hard to undermine Johnson's tolerant reconstruction policies.

As a response to Stanton's dismissal, the House voted to impeach Johnson for violating the Tenure of Office Act, which blocked the president from removing certain government officials without the consent of the Senate. Although Johnson survived the trial, his political career was over. He was not allowed to be nominated for reelection, and so he retired to Greenville, Tennessee.

ULYSSES S. GRANT

18TH PRESIDENT: 1869 - 1877

Grant was born in the Ohio countryside, where his father owned a successful leather-tanning business. Grant was very good at handling horses. When he was seventeen, he received an appointment to the U.S. Military Academy at West Point. Later in his army career, he developed a drinking problem, which forced him to resign. When he was thirty-nine, he started clerking in a small-town store. Three years later, in 1864, Grant was a lieutenant general in command of all the U.S. armies. In 1868 he was elected as the 18th President of the United States. He served two terms, and then seven years after he left office, he went bankrupt once again. He had possibly the strangest, up and down career of any American president.

In fact, his name wasn't even Ulysses S Grant. When he went to West Point, the congressman who appointed him to the military academy thought his first two names were Ulysses Simpson. Simpson was his mother's maiden name; his real names were Hiram Ulysses. So, Ulysses S. Grant was the name under which he was registered at West Point, and the name stuck.

As a young lieutenant, Grant served under General Zachary Taylor in the Mexican War. He admired General Taylor in battle and the sloppy way he dressed. He later adopted this demeanor of dress. Grant was married shortly after the Mexican War, but when he was ordered to duty in the West, he could not take his family with him, so he began to drink. Finally, his commanding officer told him he must either quit drinking or resign. And so, he resigned.

Back home, his wife's father gave him land to farm near St. Louis. He liked to farm, but the land was poor, and he couldn't make a living. He moved to St. Louis to get a job in real estate, and he failed at that too. He bounced around from job to job for some time. Finally, when the Civil War began in 1861, the North desperately needed trained officers. Grant was appointed a colonel in the army and rose to be a general. In March of 1864, President Lincoln put him in command of all northern armies. Grant turned out to be a great military leader as he had a bulldog quality to him. He knew what he wanted, and he went for it. The Union armies had more men and more equipment than the Confederates, and Grant used that to his advantage. Grant's victories brought an end to the Civil War and made him a national hero. The Republicans nominated him for President in 1868 even though he had never really been interested in politics. In fact, he had only voted for President once in his life. Despite that, he was overwhelmingly elected.

Grant inherited the reconstruction from Andrew Johnson, which dominated his first term in office. With that also came a Congress with its own ideas and policies. Due to laws enacted by the Republicans in Congress, federal troops currently controlled nearly every aspect of life in the South. Grant understood this but also believed that the federal government could not force white southerners to accept a way of life that they despised, which put him in a difficult position.

Grant was often unsure of which decision was right and let others make difficult policy decisions for him. Although Grant was incorruptible, the officials whom he appointed were not honest men. As a result, Grants administration was rocked early by corruption scandals.

The dishonesty in Washington was similar to that in the rest of the country. Ruthless people all over-exploited a weak society due to the Civil War. At the same time, the country's most successful industrialists were making vast fortunes exploiting workers and consumers. These men included Cornelius Vanderbilt, John D Rockefeller, and Andrew Carnegie. They manipulated laws and lawmakers to increase their own wealth and power.

The first scandal involving Grant's administration took place in September of 1869, during his first six months in office. It began when two of the wealthy industrialists, James Fisk and Jay Gould, tried to corner the gold market by buying up enough gold to control its supply and thereby raise its price. Their plan had one problem, which was that the federal government controlled the largest supply of gold in the country. If the scheme were to work, Fisk and Gould would have to keep the government's gold off the market. They paid Grant's brother-in-law to use his influence to do just that.

When Grant realized what was happening, he ordered the Treasury Secretary to sell four million dollars' worth of gold from the government's reserves. The sale ruined Fisk and Gould's plan, but it also sent the price of gold plummeting, which triggered a financial panic. This tarnished Grant's reputation and the day of this gold rush became known as Black Friday.

Grant attempted to move on from the scandal by returning the focus of his administration to reconstruction. He was able to pass a number of bills that gave him the power to enforce civil rights laws in the South. He used the Force Act of 1870 and the Ku Klux Klan Act of 1871 to threaten southern states with military action unless they stopped harassing the freedmen and denying them the right to vote.

Until the passage of these laws, the federal government had to rely on local authorities to control the Klan, which had not worked well. Many local police officers were themselves Klan members, so they were not going to police themselves. Just as the presidential campaign of 1872 was starting up, another scandal broke involving the Union Pacific Railroad.

By 1872, there was a massive amount of capital invested in the nation's railroads, which reached nearly three billion dollars. So much federal money was being funneled into railroad construction that major stockholders in the Union Pacific Railroad decided to form a second company to steal some of it. To make their plan work, they bribed some congressmen by selling them shares of stock at half the market price. When the press broke the story of the scandal, Congress appointed a committee to investigate. Among those implicated were Vice President Schuyler Colfax and Representative James Garfield. Although investigators found no evidence that Grant had been involved, many people believed that the scandal was a result of his incompetence.

His poor luck continued during his second term when the nation suffered one of the worst financial depressions in history. For several years, the U.S. had no private reserves for the economy, since it was still paying off its Civil War debt.

When the large banking house of Jay Cooke and Company failed in 1873, the stock market collapsed along with it. The Panic of 1873 lasted for five years and put three million people out of work while forcing thousands of small companies out of business. While the country was still dealing with this depression, Treasury Secretary William Richardson became the focus of the next Grant administration scandal. Richardson had appointed his friend Sanborn to collect some overdue federal taxes. This was typically a difficult and unrewarding job. Still, Richardson made an astonishing and illegal deal with Sanborn, allowing him to keep half of all the money he collected. By the time Congress got around to his investigation, he had already pocketed two hundred thousand dollars. Richardson was forced to resign, and Grant was embarrassed once again.

Another scandal took place when Richardson's replacement had uncovered another scheme to cheat the government. This involved federal officials who, instead of collecting liquor taxes for the government, had been keeping the money and dividing it among themselves and the distillers. Frustrated by the constant scandals, Grant demanded action, and he instructed the federal prosecutor to arrest everyone involved.

While these Grant appointees were using their power to get richer, the U.S. economy suffered. For those who still had jobs, they were making next to nothing. In large cities, thousands of homeless people crowded into police stations for shelter. Eventually, the poor demanded change, and riots began.

In between scandals that plagued his office, Congress passed the Civil Rights Act of 1875, which was the last major part of the Radical Republican legislation during reconstruction. It guaranteed blacks the civil rights currently being denied them in the South. It integrated hotels, theaters, restaurants, and business owners could no longer keep blacks out or segregate them into back rooms. It was poorly enforced and eventually was declared unconstitutional by the Supreme Court in 1883.

Despite the myriad of scandals that blemished his time in office, many people still wanted Grant to run for a third term. No president had ever done that before, and Grant wasn't about to become the first. He felt that he had been president long enough. He had entered the White House as an honest and good man, but as president, he had neither resolved key issues of a reconstruction or set high enough standards of the people he appointed to his cabinets.

By the end of Grants' second term, the U.S. had developed one of the greatest industrial economies in the world. It produced more coal, iron ore, steel, and oil than any other nation. This change drew many immigrants to the United States to work in these new factories. This drastically changed the ethnicity of the country, and it became a "melting pot."

Grant left office in 1877, and after a trip around the world, he settled in Manhattan. He invested all of his money in a brokerage firm founded by his son. This venture ended up in scandal too and eventually bankrupted the Grants. At this time, Grant learned that he had developed cancer in his throat. Determined to provide for his family before he died, Grant set to work on his memoirs. A month before he died, he moved to Mount McGregor in the Adirondacks. While unable to speak or eat regularly, he sat on the porch and raced to finish his book.

He finished his manuscript, and a week later, he died. The memoirs, published by his friend Mark Twain, sold five hundred thousand copies and restored his family's wealth. It not only made a fortune for his family, but it also turned out to be a very good and honest book.

RUTHERFORD B. HAYES

19TH PRESIDENT: 1877 - 1881

Rutherford B Hayes was born in Delaware, Ohio. His father passed away before he was born, so Rutherford was raised by his mother and her brother. Early on, he dreamed of holding public office. He studied hard in school and graduated from Kenyon College and Harvard Law School.

When he first opened his law office in Cincinnati, he had few clients. In order to save money, he slept in his office, but after winning a few large cases, he had more work than he could handle. When the Civil War started, he was appointed captain of volunteers. He had no military training; he was wounded four times and had four horses killed under him. Before the war was over, he became a major general.

Hayes was still in the army when the Republican party asked him to run for Congress. He refused to go home and campaign. Hayes said that any officer who left his post to run for political office, "aught to be scalped." He was elected anyway but stayed with the army until the war was over. He served two terms in Congress, then was elected governor of Ohio. He helped get blacks the right to vote and also helped start Ohio State University.

As the presidential election of 1876 drew near, most people thought the Democrats were sure to win. The Republican administration under Grant was marred with corruption. The party itself was divided, and some hoped to keep things as they were. Others thought the only chance to win was to have a candidate known for his honesty represent them. This group nominated Rutherford B Hayes.

The Democratic candidate was Samuel Tilden. When the election ended, Tilden had 4,284,020 votes, and Hayes had 4,036,572. These were popular votes; the electoral college was the one that would cast the final vote, which Tilden had 184, and Hayes had 165. The votes of four states, which amounted to twenty votes in all, were contested or disputed. Both the Democrats and Republicans claimed them.

The states of Florida, South Carolina, and Louisiana were in the South. Even though the Civil War had been over for eleven years, there was still a great deal of argument over who could and could not vote. Both the Democrats and the Republicans claimed to have won. If Tilden got one single vote from any of these states, he would win the election. But Hayes swept the votes and received them all.

In Congress, the argument went on for months. The time for the new president to take office was drawing near, and nobody knew who the new president would be. Finally, a deal was made where the Democrats agreed to accept a decision made by a committee. The committee was to have eight Republicans and seven Democrats. As expected, the committee voted eight to seven to give all the votes to Hayes, which made him the 19th President of the United States.

Hayes began his term with difficulty due to the Compromise of 1877, which had robbed the president of much authority. Many people speculated the election was rigged and considered him a fraud. Even though he had a sterling history, he was never able to overcome the bad impression that he made in going along with the compromise.

As part of the arrangement making Hayes president, southern Democrats demanded that the Republicans end reconstruction immediately. They wanted the federal troops out of the south that was protecting the freedmen. Having almost no choice, Hayes agreed. One of his first acts as president was to remove the last federal troops from the South, ending a decade of Radical Republican control. Southerners were overjoyed, but their former slaves weren't happy. This meant that power returned in the South to those who believed in the superiority of the white race.

In California, gangs of Irish immigrants began attacking Chinese immigrants. The Chinese had come to America to work in California's gold mines and on the railroad crews, building new transcontinental lines. At first, they were given only the lowest paying jobs that no other Americans wanted. They jumped at the chance to work, and by 1877, Chinese immigrants made up nearly 10% of the California population.

The trouble began when the gold mines began closing, and railroad construction tapered off. This forced the Chinese to begin competing with Irish Americans for the same jobs. The Chinese often got jobs because they were willing to work for less. This angered the Irish, who believed that they were entitled to the jobs because they had come to America first.

The conflict came to a head in San Francisco, where Irish American gangs beat and killed Chinese Americans on the street. Congress's response was to pass a bill banning Chinese immigration entirely. Hayes thought that this approach would hurt relations with China, so he vetoed the bill. He decided that Secretary of State William Evarts negotiate the Treaty of 1880, which limited Chinese immigration at an acceptable rate to the Chinese government.

The greatest success of Hayes's term in office was his 'hard money' policy. In order to help finance the Civil War, the Government had issued paper money called greenbacks. They were soft or 'easy' money because they weren't backed by gold, meaning they couldn't be redeemed for gold coins. In 1875, Congress had passed the Resumption of Specie Act, which required the government to take the greenbacks out of circulation and resume backing paper money with gold.

Farmers with mortgages and other debtors wanted easy money because of that encouraged inflation.

With more money in circulation, each dollar was worthless, and their debts became cheaper to pay off. Hayes overruled, and the government resumed specie payments in January.

Hayes' other initiative was civil service reform. Civil servants are the government's civilian workers. Hayes believed that federal jobs shouldn't be used as political rewards for friends, so he issued an executive order barring civil servants from taking part in politics. He also supported the efforts to develop competitive exams for hiring and promotion. Unfortunately, Congress did not agree to such a large scale of reform.

When Hayes accepted the Republican nomination, he announced he would only serve one term. Four years later, he had not changed his mind, and he retired. Because of Congress, Hayes did not make all of the reforms he would have liked, but he did leave the federal government more honest than he found it. He went back to his home in Ohio and lived out his days.

JAMES A. GARFIELD
20TH PRESIDENT: 1881

James Garfield's father was a farmer in Ohio. He died before James was two years old, and his mother and older brother raised young James. They were very poor, and he had little chance to get an education.

Garfield decided he wanted to go to school while also working any kind of job that would leave him time for his studies. He learned rapidly, and soon, one of his favorite tricks was to write Latin with one hand and Greek with the other at the same time. Before he turned thirty, he became president of a small college.

By this time, the whole nation was becoming more and more worried about slavery. Garfield believed slavery was immoral, and so he began making speeches against letting the western territories become slave states.

When the Civil War began, Garfield raised a group of volunteer soldiers, many of which had been his students. He had no military training, but he knew how to learn. He studied everything he could find on military tactics and became an excellent officer. When he turned thirty-one, he was made the youngest brigadier general in the army.

He was also elected to Congress to represent Ohio. He refused to leave the army at first, but President Lincoln talked him into quitting the army and into taking his seat in Congress, where he could serve a greater purpose. For the next eighteen years, he served in Congress. During this time, there were many corrupt politicians serving in office. They believed the purpose of government was to make the politicians and their friends rich. This was especially true during the administration of President Grant.

Garfield was accused of taking bribes, although he was never proved to have done so. In 1880 there were three well-known men in the Republican party who were trying to get the presidential nomination. At the nomination convention, none of them could get a majority vote until finally, Garfield was nominated as a compromise.

During his campaign, the Democrats often talked about the bribes Garfield was said to have taken in Congress, but they could not prove anything, and Garfield won an easy victory becoming the 20th President of the United States.

Most Americans did not expect much out of Garfield, and they assumed his presidency would be full of scandal. Garfield was determined to prove them wrong. During his first week in office, the new postmaster general found evidence of criminal wrongdoing in the post office. Instead of covering it up, Garfield ordered a full investigation.

Garfield had only been in office a few months when he was shot by a man named Charles Giteau. When he shot President Garfield, he claimed he did so because Garfield had refused to give him a job. During the long weeks that followed the shooting, while he struggled for his life, his popularity rose every day. On a number of occasions, he would seem to be improving, but due to the poor state of medical science at the time, he did not recover, and he died.

The entire nation was in shock at the death of the president. As a result of his death, people began to demand for a more honest government. They demanded better civil service laws that would keep honest government workers on the job, and because the people demanded it, Congress finally did improve the civil service laws.

CHESTER A. ARTHUR
21ST PRESIDENT: 1881 - 1885

*C*hester Arthur's father was a Baptist minister who served eleven different parishes in Vermont and New York. Because Chester moved around with his father so often, he did not settle down until he enrolled in Union College in 1845. As a student there, he took part in his fair share of pranks, once dumping the school bell into the Erie Canal. Soon after moving to New York City and becoming a lawyer in 1845, Arthur agreed to represent a black woman, Lizzie Jennings. Ms. Jennings wanted to sue a streetcar company because she had been forced to leave one of its cars that were "whites-only." Arthur eventually won the case, which ended the radical segregation of public transportation in New York City.

Arthur was interested in politics, but he did not run for office himself. Instead, he worked with political "bosses." These were men who tried to control elections by giving jobs and money to people who would vote the way the bosses wanted. In time, Arthur became an essential political boss himself.

After the Civil War, President Grant appointed Arthur the collector of the Port of New York, which was a critical position. He used it to give jobs to people who would vote and work for the Republican party. They, in turn, would have to give part of their pay to the Republican party. They also had to vote the way they were told. Arthur was not the only person doing this type of thing; it was quite common under President Grant's campaign as well. After Grant's second term, Rutherford B. Hayes became president and said that men who held important positions should not take part in the management of political parties. Arthur refused to obey, and as a result, Hayes forced him out of his job.

In 1880, the Republican party was split into two groups, one called the Stalwarts, favored Ulysses S. Grant for a third term as president was in opposition to reconciling with the South. The other was the Half-Breeds who wanted a candidate who would insist on reform and a more honest government. Arthur was a Stalwart, and he worked hard to have Grant nominated, however, some Republicans were concerned Grant's nomination would reopen fissures within the party and that a third term would set an unwise precedent. At the nominating convention those who opposed Grand general backed either Maine Senator James Blaine or Secretary of the Treasury John Sherman. However, neither commanded wide support and so when the convention deadlocked the anti-Gran faction united around James Garfield who, despite his own reluctance to become a candidate, won the nomination. As a compromise Chester Arthur, a Stalwart, was nominated for vice president, which he was then appointed to.

As President, Garfield wanted to reform the civil service and thought people should have to take a written exam to get a government job. This way, the jobs would go to those who were qualified, not just friends of influential politicians. Vice President Arthur was openly opposed and wanted things left as they were.

Garfield was only in office for a couple of months when he was murdered by a man named Charles

Giteau. When Giteau shot the President, he shouted, "I am a Stalwart! Arthur is now president!" He later said he shot President Garfield because he had refused to give him a job.

With Garfield's death Chester A. Arthur became the 21st President of the United States. The entire nation was shocked at the president's murder and especially for the reason he died. Many were frightened and wondered what Arthur would be like as President. Some Stalwart politicians were happy to have him as president because they thought things would go back to the way they had been under Grant. Arthur did not forget that Garfield had been murdered by a man who violently supported the Stalwarts and all that they stood for. A change came over Arthur, and he realized that as president, his duty was to all the people, not just to one party. His cronies soon came to Washington looking for jobs, but Arthur sent them away. He stated, "For the vice presidency, I am indebted to Mr. Conkling, but for the presidency of the United States, my debt is to the Almighty." There would be no payoffs to his friends.

In 1882, Arthur proved he meant what he said by vetoing the Rivers and Harbors Act. This bill, funded nineteen million dollars' worth of unnecessary construction projects and was an obvious example of spending designed to benefit the districts of the most powerful congressmen. His veto was overridden by Congress, but he still won praise for taking a stand against wasteful spending.

Arthur signed the Chinese Exclusion Act of 1882, which halted immigration for ten years and kept the Chinese already in the United States from becoming citizens. This law placed the first significant restrictions on immigration to the United States. It also broke the Treaty of 1880 with China.

In 1883, Arthur signed the most important legislation of his administration, the Pendleton Act. This permanently reformed the civil service. No longer would Americans believe that the civil service was filled only with politically connected people who did little or no work. It was due to President Garfield's assassination that this was possible. Since his assassin was seeking a government job at the time, the public assumed he was linked to corrupt civil service. This helped promote reform. The Pendelton Act created competitive examinations for government jobs and also established the Civil Service Commission.

This changed the way political parties were funded, and it was not necessarily an improvement. They were no longer able to rely on party-appointed civil servants for their money; they had to look for other avenues in order to fund their campaigns. They turned to big businesses, and in return, they expected favors. Huge companies such as Rockefeller's Standard Oil and Carnegie's U.S. Steel had been looking eagerly for ways to influence lawmakers. Both political parties were equally eager to accept their cash.

Arthur went on to work hard and help bring the Navy up to date with modern ships. He changed the postal system to give better and cheaper service. The Stalwart politicians did not forgive him for turning his back on them, and they refused to nominate him for President in 1884. Little did they know that he had an incurable disease and thought he might die in office anyway, which could have given him the courage to act so defiantly.

After his presidency, he went back to his home in New York to live out his days with many admirers.

GROVER CLEVELAND

22ND PRESIDENT: 1885 - 1889

Grover Cleveland grew up a strong boy who loved fishing and being outdoors. In school, he was an average student, but he was a hard worker and planned to attend college. When he was sixteen, his father passed away, forcing him to find a job instead. He worked for a year in New York City before being offered a full scholarship to college if he agreed to become a Presbyterian minister as his father had been. Although he wanted a formal education, he turned down the offer and decided to head west. He made it to Buffalo, where he met up with an uncle who arranged for him to work in his law office while studying law. By the time he was twenty-two, he was a lawyer.

When the Civil War started, Grover and his two brothers drew straws to see who would go off to war and who would stay home and take care of their mother. Grover drew the short straw and kept working. Later in life, his political enemies would say he stayed out of the army because he was afraid. Still, anyone who knew Grover, knew this was not true.

He went on to become a very successful lawyer, and in 1881 he was asked by the Democratic party to run for mayor of Buffalo. Most of the people there were Republicans, but they were unhappy with how the city was run. They wanted a change and a more honest and reliable government. He was elected and gave the people an even more honest government than some had anticipated. He reorganized the city so that it ran under budget. Hi fired anyone he caught taking bribes, and within a year he had cleaned it up. Since he had such an exceptional record cleaning up corruption and saving the taxpayers money, the Democrats nominated him for governor. With a sterling reputation, he was quickly voted into office without ever making a single campaign speech.

As governor, Cleveland made sure the state received its money for every penny spent. Some of the politicians did not like his practices, but the people sure did. In 1884, Cleveland was nominated by the Democrats to run for president. No Democrat had been elected president since the Civil War. At this time, there was a faction of the Republican Party called the Mugwumps who were political activists and intensely opposed political corruption. The Mugwumps were demanding reform and a more honest government and because they did not like the Republican candidate, they voted for Cleveland instead. It was very close, but Cleveland won and became the 22nd President of the United States.

Cleveland was not well known around the country. Even in Washington, people were unsure of who he was. His trip to the capital for his inauguration was only his second time visiting the city. The crowd that gathered to see him was the largest he had ever seen. Cleveland rose to the occasion and knew he had a job to do. In the beginning, he tried to go at it alone. He worked without a secretary and even answered the White House telephone himself from time to time. Since he had great attention to detail, he knew more about the issues of the day than any of his opponents. He was very studious and sometimes got so caught up in the specifics of an issue that he lost his perspective.

The new president was rather blunt and had a hot temper. He made few friends in Washington while making many enemies. He knew that he wanted a hands-off government. He believed that people should support the government and not the other way around. In 1887, when a severe drought hit Texas, causing crop failures, Congress passed a bill to distribute free seed to farms so they could replant. While the bill was very popular, Cleveland vetoed it because he believed the people should be wary of the government rather than looking to it for handouts.

Due to his attitude, Cleveland was not part of the shaping of congressional legislation. He either signed bills or vetoed them. One of the most important bills he signed was the Interstate Commerce Act of 1887. Railroads had been able to charge passengers and shippers whatever they wanted, and often these rates were extremely high. Most railroads used practices such as rebates to favor large corporations over smaller companies. The Interstate Commerce Act was passed to ensure that all railroads charged "reasonable and just" rates. This was the first regulatory agency ever established by Congress.

Cleveland used his veto power most aggressively when it came to bills that he considered abuse on the Treasury. Among these bills were ones introduced to provide special pensions for certain Union army veterans. Cleveland agreed that the government was obligated to provide pensions for soldiers who had been injured in battle. He worried that the prospect of easy pension money was leading to a great deal of fraud.

Many corrupt lawyers would file false claims on behalf of Union veterans who were perfectly healthy. Sometimes the Pension Bureau accepted these claims without any investigation. Other times the bureau investigated and rejected them. However, even then, an influential veteran could still persuade his congressman to force them to pay. Because of this, pensions were given to criminals, deserters, and even men who had never fought in the army. To put an end to this cheating, Cleveland began reading each and every one of the private bills, which numbered in the hundreds, and he vetoed nearly all.

Towards the end of his first term in office, he challenged Congress to reduce tariff rates. The rates were raised during the Lincoln administration to pay for the Civil War and had remained high ever since. After the war, the rates had remained in place to protect developing U.S. industries. Still, they had also pushed up prices and created a massive federal surplus. This made Congressmen eager to spend the money on pork-barrel projects in their home states. Rather than allowing this, Cleveland demanded that Congress lower the tariff rates. There was a strong adverse reaction to this demand. Big business wanted to stay insulated from foreign competition. The response was so vehemently against Cleveland that it may have cost him reelection.

BENJAMIN HARRISON

23RD PRESIDENT: 1889 - 1893

*B*orn in Ohio at the home of William Henry Harrison, his grandfather was elected president. Benjamin's childhood was typical of a farm boy at that time. He gathered wood and water, fed the cattle on the six-hundred-acre farm. He enjoyed hunting and fishing as well. By the time he was twenty-one, he had graduated from college and married. He moved to Indianapolis with his bride and became a successful lawyer.

When the Civil War began, Harrison formed a regiment of volunteers. He was appointed colonel, and his regiment took part in many battles. He proved to be a good officer, and after the war, he went back to Indianapolis to continue practicing law. In January of 1881, Harrison was elected to the Senate. His father had been a congressman, and his grandfather had been president, so his name was well known throughout the country. It was partly for this reason that in 1888 the Republicans nominated him for president.

Harrison was short, only five feet and six inches tall. During the Civil war, his soldiers affectionately called him Little Ben. He was often fixated on only one subject at a time. Sometimes he would walk past people he knew without recognizing them, and because of this, people said he was cold and unfriendly. He was not a man of the people in the sense that he enjoyed meeting big crowds of strangers. He was very formal, and his personality lacked warmth. Some people called him a "human iceberg." Instead, he ran what was called a "front porch" campaign. He stayed at home and talked with small groups of politicians who came to see him.

It was a very close race running against Grover Cleveland, but Harrison received more electoral votes and became the 23rd President of the United States.

During the Gilded Age, corporations had created monopolies in a number of industries. Rockefeller had formed the Standard Oil trust to corner the oil market legally. In his inaugural address, Harrison warned that trusts such as Standard Oil needed to play by the rules of freed trade or else face government discipline. When the trusts ignored his warning, Congress passed the first antitrust law in 1890.

The Sherman Anti-Trust Act, which was sponsored by Senator John Sherman, made it a crime to limit trade in the form of a trust or otherwise. This meant that men such as Rockefeller could no longer control or combine several companies in order to monopolize an industry. Lawyers were able to find several ways around the law in time.

Navy Secretary Benjamin Tracy continued the huge shipbuilding program that had begun during the Cleveland administration. This modernization of the navy fit well with Harrison's plan to expand U.S. influence in Latin America and the Pacific region.

He favored an aggressive foreign policy and helped arrange the first Pan-American Conference. This conference expanded the U.S. presence in Latin America while reducing that of Great Britain. His specific goal was to control the narrow Isthmus of Panama, and one day, have the U.S. build a canal linking the Atlantic Ocean to the Pacific.

In the Pacific, U.S. minister to Hawaii landed troops to protect business leaders who had recently rebelled against Queen Liliuokalani. After overthrowing her native government and setting up their own regime, which were mostly sugar growers, asked for the immediate annexation of Hawaii by the United States. State Department representatives negotiated a treaty of annexation during the president's final weeks in office.

Harrison inherited a large Treasury surplus caused by high tariff rates. Republicans and Democrats both wanted to eliminate the surplus, but they disagreed as to how. The Democrats wanted to lower tariff rates, which would take in less money. Harrison and the Republicans wanted to keep the high rates and spend the surplus. Harrison signed the Dependent and Disability Pensions Act of 1890. Harrison had been a general during the Civil War and had great sympathy for his fellow veterans. The Act showered money on them in the form of pensions for all Union veterans who were now unable to work for any reason at all. Their injuries did not even have to be battle-related.

Meanwhile, the new silver discoveries in Arizona and Nevada had created a large number of boomtowns. The silver became less valuable because the market could only absorb so much of the metal. To keep its price high, miners lobbied the government to buy more silver by issuing more paper money. Farmers in the South and West supported this idea since it would lead to inflation, which would make their debts easier to pay off.

In the East, bankers who controlled the government's monetary policy were terrified at the thought of unlimited silver coinage. They needed the support of the South and West to pass a new tariff bill, so they agreed to a compromise. The Sherman Silver Purchase Act of 1890 committed the government to buy 4.5 million ounces of silver each month, which was nearly the entire output of the western mines. Around the same time, the McKinley Tariff Act of 1890 completed the deal for both sides.

The McKinley Tariff Act of 1890 was a highly protective measure that raised tariff rates to 48 percent, which was the highest peacetime level ever. The bill backfired. The point of the high tariff was to make foreign goods expensive so that Americans would be more likely to buy domestic goods. Still, greedy manufacturers just raised their prices to match those of foreign goods.

American consumers were irate, and they turned their anger on the Republicans in office. Many were voted out of office during the 1890 midterm. Many voters turned against Harrison, and he was defeated for reelection in 1892. Harrison went back to his home in Indianapolis. He wrote books about the United States government and continued to practice law until his death in 1901.

GROVER CLEVELAND

4th President: 1893 - 1897

Grover Cleveland was the only president ever to be reelected after being voted out of office. He returned to the White House, determined to lower tariff rates. Before he could accomplish that, the Panic of 1893 hit, and the depression that followed lasted throughout his entire second term.

The financial panic began before he ever took office. In 1893 the Philadelphia & Reading Railroad went out of business. Soon other railroads followed, and by 1896, one-quarter of the nation's rail lines were out of business. Comprised of nearly one-million workers, U.S. railroads had been the country's largest employer, and financing railroads had been the biggest business on Wall Street. The bankruptcies put hundreds of thousands of people out of work, and the stock market came to a halt. Many of the people that lost their jobs also lost their homes. While Cleveland wanted to help these people, his belief in a "hands-off" government kept him from proposing any relief programs. He focused on keeping the economy steady until the depression passed.

This largest crisis facing the government was the run on its gold reserves. Due to the Sherman Silver Purchase Act, the government had to buy large amounts of silver from the west each year with paper money, which could be exchanged for gold. When people began using this law as a way to trade silver for gold, the government's gold supply quickly dropped. Soon the Treasury had less than one hundred million dollars in gold left.

Cleveland's first move was to call an emergency session of Congress to repeal the Sherman Silver Purchase Act. This caused a fight that developed between conservatives, who favored the gold standard, and populists, who wanted free coinage of silver. Keeping the gold standard meant that U.S. currency would continue to be backed by only gold, while free coinage of silver meant that money could be backed by either gold or silver, thereby increasing the supply.

Putting more dollars into circulation would force down the value of each one. The prospect of inflation pleased southern and western farmers who didn't have much cash. At the same time, it angered eastern bankers, who did. This created a divide in the Democratic party between the "gold bugs" and the populist "silverites." In the end, a repeal of the Sherman Silver Purchase Act was put in place, but this did not stop the gold drainage. Now more desperate than ever, Cleveland was forced to ask Wall Street for help. At his request, J.P. Morgan organized a group of New York bankers to come to the treasury's aid. They made a loan of sixty-two million dollars in gold, which halted the drain and stabilized the economy by restoring people's faith in the financial system. Morgan and his friends made a lot of money on the deal, which caused the populists to claim that the president had sold out to Wall Street.

Large corporations used the depression as an excuse to lower workers' wages even further. The worker's quality of life was already quite low, and now these additional cuts provoked some aggressive and violent retaliation. After the Civil War, manufacturing companies grew larger and more powerful. They forced their workers, especially their immigrant workers, to accept lower wages and work longer hours in more dangerous conditions. The only escape for people trapped in this environment was to join the Union.

The Union's principal weapon was the strike. During the late nineteenth century, most large companies responded to strikes by hiring thugs to beat up the striking workers. With the government on their side, the company bosses usually won.

President Cleveland was so preoccupied with the economic situation that he didn't' get around to tariff reform until 1894. A bill was created in the House that dramatically reduced tariff rates, but the bill was reworked in the Senate until it barely lowered them at all. President Cleveland refused to sign it and therefore failed to reduce tariff rates. Cleveland's second term ended in 1897. When he left office, despite enduring a terrible recession, the federal government was a better-working and more honest organization. His last words before he died were: "I have tried so hard to do right."

WILLIAM MCKINLEY

25TH PRESIDENT: 1897 - 1901

William McKinley was born in Niles, Ohio, a town with a population of about three hundred. When he was nine, his family moved to Poland, Ohio, which wasn't much bigger. He went to local schools then attended Allegheny College. He had been in college only a short time when he became ill and had to go home. He was eighteen years old when the Civil War began, and two months later, he enlisted as a private and fought at Antietam. For his bravery under fire, he was promoted to second lieutenant. His new commanding officer was Col. Rutherford B Hayes, the future president. Hayes once wrote about McKinley, "Young as he was, we soon found that in the business of a soldier... young McKinley showed unusual and unsurpassed capacity." After the war, he studied law. He began to practice in Canton, Ohio, and married Ida Saxton, the daughter of the local banker. His political career started after the war when he helped Hayes win election as governor of Ohio. He later ran for Congress and served there for fourteen years. He became one of the leaders of the Republican Party. He later became governor of Ohio. He had a national reputation as a businesslike executive. Then in 1896, he was nominated for president.

Similar to Benjamin Harrison, McKinley ran a "front porch" campaign. He did this because he refused to leave his wife to travel around the country for an extended period of time. The wealthy men who were backing McKinley brought people from all over the country to see him.

The Democrats claimed McKinley would take orders from the wealthy bankers in the big cities, but this did not sway his popularity. He won the election by a landslide and became the 25th President of the United States.

Similar to Cleveland, McKinley was a conservative, hands-off politician. Big business was given free rein during his term, and hugely powerful trusts were allowed to develop without much resistance. His immediate problem upon taking office was a growing budget deficit. The Supreme Court had recently ruled that a proposed income tax was unconstitutional, the government's revenues still came primarily from tariffs on imported goods. Tariff rates had been the hottest issue during the last three elections. When the Democrats were in power, they lowered the rates, but with Republicans such as McKinley in office, the rates went up. At first, the public protested because it raised prices on consumer goods. Eventually, the protests came to an end as the country soon became distracted by events taking place in Spanish-held Cuba.

The depression in the United States caused by the Panic of 1893 had decimated Cuba's sugar industry. The new tariff, which imposed a 40 percent tax on sugar, made matters even worse. By 1895, the underemployment on the island moved the desperate and poor Cubans to revolt against their Spanish colonial rulers.

The Spanish responded by imprisoning the rebels in concentration camps, where two hundred thousand people died of disease and starvation. When learning of this, Americans demanded that their government do something. At the time, Grover Cleveland was president, and he refused to interfere as tensions grew higher. When McKinley became president, he tried to avoid a fight. He was a veteran of the Civil War and knew how bloody war could be. The sinking of the Maine in the harbor of Havana made war inevitable.

The Spanish contended that the explosion was an accident, and a U.S. investigation proved inconclusive. Journalists insisted that the explosion was deliberate, and McKinley was pressured into declaring war. On April 11th, 1898, he sent a message to Congress, urging the use of military force in Cuba.

This began the Spanish-American War, which was dubbed the "splendid little war" because it was quick and relatively painless for the U.S. Only a few hundred soldiers were killed in battle. Still, several thousand more died from tropical diseases. Nearly a month after it began, seventeen thousand soldiers left Florida for Cuba, led by Theodore Roosevelt, who had just resigned as assistant secretary of the Navy. The Spanish agreed to surrender Cuba on August 12th. In the peace talks that followed, the Cubans were granted limited independence, but the

United States took possession of Puerto Rico, Guam, and the Philippines. With the annexation of Hawaii that same year, the nation was now well on its way to becoming an imperial world power. Grover Cleveland tried to restore native rule to the Hawaiian island, but the provisional government that was run by the white planters held on firmly. When McKinley replaced Cleveland, Hawaii was annexed in July of 1898.

In 1900, McKinley was elected to a second term in office. All over the country, business was improving. In 1901, while in Buffalo, New York, McKinley was shaking hands with a huge crowd of people when a man stepped up as if to shake his hand. He had a handkerchief wrapped around his right hand, and inside the handkerchief was a gun. He fired two shots killing President McKinley.

THEODORE ROOSEVELT

26TH PRESIDENT: 1901 - 1909

Theodore Roosevelt was often sick as a child. He suffered from asthma during much of his youth, which prevented him from attending school, and he often had to sleep sitting up in a chair so that he wouldn't cough all night. He decided to build up his body and exercised tirelessly. He slowly overcame his asthma and developed a very muscular body. He never went to regular school, but he did have private tutors. At eighteen, he entered Harvard University. He graduated at twenty-two and was married that same year.

His wealthy friends warned him not to go into politics because it was "a dirty business." His answer was that it didn't have to be. He joined a Republican club, and when he was twenty-three, he was elected to the state legislature. Within six weeks, he tried to get a crooked judge thrown out of office. He did not succeed, but he quickly developed a reputation as a fearless and honest politician.

In 1884 his wife and his mother both died within a few hours of each other. To distract himself from his grief, he moved to Dakota. He bought a ranch and worked as a cowboy. He spent long days in the saddle and even became a deputy sheriff that helped hunt down outlaws. He developed a reputation of being as fearless on the frontier as in the legislature.

After two years, he went back east and remarried. He served in Washington on the Civil Service Commission and in New York City as Commissioner of police. In 1897, President McKinley appointed him assistant secretary of the Navy. During this time, Cuba was fighting to become independent of Spain. Roosevelt wanted the U.S. to join in the action. He said McKinley was 'lily-livered" for not petitioning Congress to declare war on Spain. When war was finally declared, Roosevelt quit his job.

He had always been a little embarrassed that his own father had not fought in the Civil War. So he formed a cavalry regiment called the Rough Riders. It was comprised of wealthy polo players from the East and hard-riding cowboys from the West. In Cuba, Roosevelt led them in a charge up San Juan Hill to capture a Spanish fort. He later admitted that San Juan was the greatest day of his life.

After the Spanish-American War, he was elected governor of New York. He was a strong governor and was honest as well. Many politicians were afraid of him, and it was for this reason that in 1900 they nominated him for vice president. They figured that as vice president he would be out of their way with little for him to do. On September 6, 1901, President McKinley was shot and killed. At this time, Roosevelt was mountain climbing, but he quickly returned when he heard the news, and he assumed office as the 26th President of the United States.

At only forty-three years of age, he was nevertheless well prepared for the job. He was well-read and well-traveled. He was an avid reader and sometimes would read up to three books in one day. He was also very outgoing. He exercised often, and while he was governor of New York, he once wrestled the middleweight champion. As president, he kept in shape by boxing regularly with professional sparring partners. He would often invite political rivals to climb into the ring with him for a "friendly" sparring match.

One of his first acts in office was to take on the trusts. Trusts were companies that work together to limit competition in a particular industry such as steel or tobacco. The most famous trust in United States history was the Standard Oil Company run by Rockefeller. He created his trust to fix oil prices. Rockefeller understood that if he could control the supply of oil, he could set whatever price he wanted.

Political leaders who protected working people against big business were referred to as Progressives. They opposed trusts because of the unfair practices used to drive smaller companies out of business. They thought that breaking up the trusts would result in more competition and better prices for all.

In his first speech addressing Congress, President Roosevelt stated that the most ruthless trusts needed to be reformed. However, there was a lot of political support for trusts, even within Roosevelt's own party.

In March of 1902, he brought suit against a railroad trust called the Northern Securities Company, which shocked many bankers on Wall Street but greatly pleased the public. His knowledge of Wall Street was helpful in understanding how to deal with them. His father had been a wealthy merchant who had served on many corporate boards of directors. As a result, he knew on a personal level most of the important business leaders in the U.S.

He did not want to "bust" all of the trusts, only those that were the worst offenders. He believed that taking no action would lead Congress to enact more radical measures in the future. He called his middle ground the Square Deal. When his case finally made it to court, the court ruled against the trust and for Roosevelt's case. This was an important victory for Roosevelt's antitrust policy.

During his first term, the most severe domestic crisis involved the anthracite coal miners in Pennsylvania who went on strike for better wages and working conditions. Up until that time, presidents mostly sided with business owners against striking workers. Still, Roosevelt had a different opinion on the matter. He sensed that times had changed and that the public valued fair treatment for workers. One of his first moves was to send in federal troops but not to break up the strike. He said they were being sent to protect the mine owner's property, but in reality, they were there to protect the striking miners from thugs hired by the mine owners.

Roosevelt invited both sides to Washington, where he helped labor and management resolve their differences peacefully. The strikers won some concessions, and Roosevelt's popularity soared. The success of his antitrust and pro-labor policies made it clear that Roosevelt's government would protect the interests of the public against greedy business practices.

Roosevelt's motto was, "Speak softly and carry a big stick." This carried over into international policy as well, which he called Big Stick Diplomacy.

In 1823, President James Monroe had warned European nations against further colonization in the Western Hemisphere. At this time, the government of the Dominican Republic was deeply in debt to a few European nations, mainly Italy and France. These countries were threatening to take over the Dominican government if the debt wasn't repaid immediately. In a speech to Congress, Roosevelt repeated that the United States would not tolerate any European intervention in the Americas. In 1904, Roosevelt added to the Monroe Doctrine in what became known as the Roosevelt Corollary, which is a statement that logically follows from a previous agreement. The Roosevelt Corollary gave him the right to intervene in the affairs of any Latin American country that proved incapable of governing itself.

Critics argued that it would lead to U.S. imperialism. Roosevelt's supporters argued that the corollary was simply common sense. The world was a dangerous place, and we were best suited to police Latin America. It was clear that Roosevelt was establishing American leadership in the world as no president had before.

One of Roosevelt's more memorable achievements in his first term was the Panama Canal. When he first began working on the project, the canal zone still belonged to the nation of Colombia, and the Colombian government didn't want to sell. Later, revolution broke out in Panama, and Roosevelt backed the rebels, and with U.S. help, they won their independence. Afterward, Panama gratefully sold the canal zone to Roosevelt on the same terms that the Colombians had initially rejected. The next fall, Roosevelt had an overwhelming victory for reelection.

The Russo-Japanese War began in 1904 when the Japanese army launched a surprise attack on Russian troops. For months, President Roosevelt worked to stop the fighting. He proposed a number of ceasefire plans, but Russia and Japan couldn't agree on a formula for peace. Eventually, in 1905, Roosevelt announced a breakthrough, and the two warring nations agreed to accept the plan for peace.

Formal talks began in New Hampshire, and three weeks later, the Russian and Japanese delegations agreed to a treaty ending the war. Roosevelt was thrilled, and Russia and Japan gave Roosevelt plenty of credit for his assistance. In 1906, Roosevelt became the first American to win a Nobel Prize when he won the Nobel Prize for Peace. It was highly unusual for a U.S. president to be so active in world affairs. Presidents generally tried to stay out of European and Asian disputes. This was a sign that the U.S. was becoming a world power.

Roosevelt refused to run for a third term, and instead, he went big game hunting in Africa. He toured Europe. He wrote books and made speeches, he still wanted to stay busy. He was not happy with the way President Taft was running the country, and in 1912, he once more ran for President. Since Taft was the Republican candidate, Roosevelt formed a new party called the Progressive Party. While Roosevelt was in Milwaukee to make a campaign speech, he was shot by an insane man. He was only wounded, and he finished his speech before going to the hospital. When a reporter asked how he felt, Roosevelt said, "I feel as strong as a bull moose." From then on, his party was known as the Bull Moose Party.

In this election, the Republican vote was split between Taft and Roosevelt. Because of this, the Democratic candidate was elected. Roosevelt went back to his home on Long Island. He wrote his autobiography as well as many magazine articles. He went to South America as well and spent months exploring an unknown river called the River of Doubt. He got jungle fever and almost died. By this time, he was blind in one eye and would never fully recover. He passed away quietly in his sleep in 1919.

WILLIAM H. TAFT

27TH PRESIDENT: 1909 - 1913

*E*ven as a young boy, William Taft was big. His brothers and sisters called him Big Lub. Others called him Big Bill. He grew to be about six feet tall and weighed close to three hundred pounds. He was a good tennis player and a surprisingly good dancer. He loved to play baseball, and he hit with power but was a slow baserunner. After his graduation from Yale and the University of Cincinnati College of Law, Taft used his father's political connections to get a job as an assistant county prosecutor. In 1887 the governor of Ohio appointed Taft to the state supreme court and then went on to become a judge.

In 1901 Taft was appointed the civil governor of the Philippines, which then belonged to the United

States. In 1904, President Theodore Roosevelt appointed Taft secretary of war. He did an excellent job. Roosevelt was often away but never had any worries because Big Bill Taft was "sitting on the lid." It was primarily because of Roosevelt that the Republican party nominated Taft for President in 1908. Taft was not excited about the idea of being president as he did not think he was qualified. He had his sight set on being appointed to the Supreme Court. Mrs. Taft wanted to be First Lady, so she talked him into running. With Roosevelt's backing, Taft was elected as the 27th President of the United States.

Taft had a tall task of following in Roosevelt's footsteps. Everyone expected him to follow along with the path Roosevelt set, and if he did things differently, he was heavily criticized. Taft began his term by appointing a new cabinet, which obviously meant that some of Roosevelts last cabinet were going to be replaced. Many newspapers interpreted this normal reshuffling as an abandonment of Roosevelt's policies. Taft was more conservative than Roosevelt. Many of Roosevelt's programs became law under Taft. His record on conservation was very good. Taft was the first president to protect federal lands on which oil had been found. He also protected land that contained coal, which was even more widely used than oil at the time, due to railroads. This went against big business which wanted to exploit those lands for profit.

Taft's trust-busting record was impressive as well. During his four years in office, he oversaw twice as many prosecutions as there had been during the seven years prior under Roosevelt.

The most famous antitrust case of the Taft years involved the Standard Oil Company. Roosevelt had ordered an investigation of their monopolistic practices before leaving office, but the case didn't reach the Supreme Court until Taft had been sworn into office. The Supreme Court found that the existence of the trust violated the Sherman Anti-Trust Act and ordered that it be broken up.

Also during his term, Congress passed the Sixteenth and Seventeenth Amendments, both of which were ratified in 1913. The Sixteenth Amendment made the income tax constitutional, and the Seventeenth Amendment provided for the direct election of senators. In the past, senators had been chosen by state legislatures instead of by the people.

His foreign policy was termed Dollar Diplomacy because he relied on financial rather than military means to promote the interests of the United States abroad. His focus was on Latin America. He encouraged U.S. bankers to invest in Honduras and Haiti, and in 1912 he resorted to military force by sending marines to Nicaragua to crush a rebellion that threatened to oust the business-friendly government.

In spite of all of these great achievements, Taft was still criticized. He was an avid golfer, so the perception was that he did nothing in the office. It just so happened that his golf partners were important business leaders, and he chose to do his meetings on the golf course. Some newspapers complained that the president shouldn't be playing a rich man's sport with people who made unfair profits at the public's expense.

The main reason for his lack of support was that he was always being compared to Roosevelt. At the beginning of Taft's presidency, Roosevelt went on a well-publicized safari in Africa. He said he wanted to hunt wild game, but he really wanted to give his friend Taft a chance to make his own mark in office.

While the paper was printing stories of Roosevelt's expedition in Africa, they would make jokes that Taft's favorite sport was eating. Even worse, in 1910, a jealous Roosevelt suggested that his support for Taft might have been a mistake. This remark set off a storm of controversy and deeply hurt Taft, who had considered Roosevelt a close friend and mentor. This put a strain on their relationship, and Taft later admitted that the loss of his friendship with Roosevelt was the hardest part of his presidency.

Roosevelt and his friends said that Taft had sold out Roosevelt's ideals. When the Republicans nominated Taft to run for a second term in 1912, Roosevelt formed the Bull Moose party to run against him. Taft lost the reelection, and when he left the White House, he said: "I am glad to be going. This is the lonesomest place in the world." He went back to his law practice. He taught law at Yale. In 1921, he was appointed Chief Justice of the United States, which was the work that he loved most. He served until his retirement because of ill health in 1930.

WOODROW WILSON

28TH PRESIDENT: 1913 - 1921

Woodrow Wilson was born in Virginia five years before the start of the Civil War. His father and grandfather were Presbyterian preachers. At one time, his father's church was turned into a hospital for wounded Confederate soldiers. He considered himself a Southerner and was proud of the fight the Confederates had made while at the same time was glad the North had won and kept the Union undivided.

He grew up lean and muscular. He played football at Princeton and later helped coach the team. He went on to receive a law degree and practiced law in Atlanta. He quickly found out that he did not enjoy law, and so he went back to school and received a

Ph.D. and started teaching. In 1902 he was made the president of Princeton University.

In 1910 he was elected governor of New Jersey. Then two years later, he was elected as the 28th President of the United States. Like Roosevelt, he believed that the job of the president was to represent all the people. Where Congressmen represented specific areas and groups, the president represented everyone. He set the tone for his presidency with his inauguration address, where he outlined the issues facing the nation in terms of what was right and wrong. He viewed his job as a moral responsibility.

He began with a lot of energy, and in his first two years, he was extremely productive. During this time, Congress passed some of the most progressive laws. During his campaign, he promised to lower tariffs, and he followed through on the promise. He passed the Underwood Tariff, which cut the average rate from 41 to 27 percent, which was the lowest rates had been since the Civil War.

Since lower tariffs meant less revenue for the government, he planned to make up the difference by establishing the first national income tax. This applied to Americans making above three thousand dollars a year, and they would have to pay 1 percent of their income to the government. The people making over twenty thousand dollars a year were required to pay an additional amount up to 6 percent. This was very controversial at the time.

Wilson also implemented the Federal Reserve Act of 1913, which reorganized the nation's banking system. It had once been a source of conflict between Alexander Hamilton and Thomas Jefferson. Forty years after that, Andrew Jackson and Nicholas Biddle fought over the re-chartering of the Second Bank. It was now 80 years later, and the public was still recovering from the system's poor performance during the Panic of 1907. Wilson's Federal Reserve Act set up a new network of twelve regional banks, each of which reported to a national board of governors that was appointed by the president. Their job was to control the supply of money available for investment.

During an economic boom, the board was supposed to raise interest rates, so that people wouldn't borrow and spend too much. During recessions, they would lower rates so that people could get the credit they needed.

During his first term, Wilson dedicated much of his attention to preventing the U.S. from becoming involved in World War I. The Germans were making it complicated. In February of 1915, the German government announced that it considered the waters around Great Britain to be a war zone. Therefore all ships in those waters, including those belonging to the U.S., would be subject to attack. Wilson immediately responded, warning the Germans that attacks on neutral U.S. ships would force him to take military action. In response to this Germany's military leadership backed down because it didn't want to bring America into the war.

By the start of his second term in 1917, President Wilson discovered he could no longer resist keeping the U.S. out of the war. He tried to remain neutral in order to broker peace. This was to no avail, and a month later, Germany announced that it would resume unrestricted submarine warfare in the waters around Great Britain. This meant that U.S. neutrality would not be respected at sea, leaving Wilson with no other option. The public was not completely sold on the idea of war until a decoded text of the Zimmerman Telegram was made public. This was a message from German foreign minister Arthur Zimmerman to his ambassador in Mexico, which had been intercepted by British intelligence. In the telegram, Zimmermann proposed an alliance between Germany and Mexico. It suggested that if the U.S. entered the war, Germany would help Mexico reconquer the "lost territories" of Texas, New Mexico, and Arizona.

Once released to the public, overwhelming support to join the fight swept the nation. For the rest of 1917, Wilson began preparations for war.

In January of 1918, Wilson gave a speech outlining the fourteen points upon which he considered peace should be made. These points included arms reduction, free navigation of the seas, and self-determination for colonies. The final point of his plan called for the formation of an ambitious League of Nations, which could avoid wars in the future by guaranteeing the rights and independence of all the world's nations.

During the spring of 1918, before the majority of U.S. troops reached Europe, Germany launched one last attack. It failed, and so did their war effort moving forward. By September of 1918, there were more than a million American soldiers in Europe, which shifted the balance of power considerably. Realizing they were overmatched, the Germans sent Wilson a note asking the president for a truce and peace talks based on the fourteen points that Wilson had outlined.

Wilson was excited for the opportunity to negotiate peace among the nations, so he decided to lead the talks himself. On his way to Paris, where the talks were to be held, the president was welcomed with a warm greeting by the Europeans, who considered him a hero. His actions in helping to end the war earned him the Nobel Peace Prize. While not all fourteen points were agreed to, the Treaty of Versailles, which the Germans were forced to sign, did create the League of Nations.

During the six months that Wilson was abroad, his health was on the decline. He also began losing control of the U.S. Government. When he returned home with his treaty, the Senate was not ready to ratify it. Wilson believed that the most essential part of the treaty was the establishment of the League of Nations, and he was prepared to defend it no matter the cost. In September of 1919, Wilson embarked on an ill-advised national speaking tour intended to rally public support for the treaty. He visited twenty-nine cities in three weeks, but since his health was on the decline, he did not make it past Colorado. He suffered a stroke that paralyzed him on his entire left side.

While trying to heal, he relied heavily on his wife Edith to determine what matters were important enough to deserve his attention. All other matters, she handled on her own. She ran the White House in his name. Wilson never offered to step down, and nobody confronted him over this unusual situation. The Senate voted in March of 1920 to reject the Treaty of Versailles, but this had little effect on Germany. The other Allies had already agreed to the treaty and were enforcing its terms. The terms of the treaty placed very severe restraint on Germany giving some German territories to neighboring countries, restricting its military capabilities and requiring it to pay significant war reparations.

Gradually Wilson recovered some of his strength back, but he was never really well again. When his second term in office ended, he decided to leave politics. Others would continue to fight for the ideals that he established.

WARREN G. HARDING
29TH PRESIDENT: 1921 - 1923

Warren G. Harding grew up on a farm in Caledonia, Ohio, where he was responsible for milking cows, tending to horses, and painting barns. He quit school at seventeen, and he and two friends purchased an almost bankrupt newspaper for three hundred dollars. He then became the sole owner of the Marion Star. He used this paper to help launch his political career, and in 1914 he was elected to the United States Senate.

Harding liked being a senator and normally voted along the Republican party lines. He also helped get his friends back home jobs and spent so much time doing so that he missed more than half of the roll calls in the Senate. He had very powerful political friends that nominated him as a candidate for president. World War I had been over for only two years, but the American people were still feeling the effects. Harding ran his platform on the promise of returning the country to normalcy. He won the election in a landslide and became the 29th President of the United States.

Harding was polar opposites of Wilson regarding his idealism. He always avoided taking a stance on the League of Nations. When he was sworn into office, he made it known that he would not support the U.S. being a member of that organization.

One of his initial moves in office was to create the Bureau of the Budget. In the past, each executive department had managed its own budget, but now the process would be unified and streamlined. He also signed into the law two new tariffs that replaced the Underwood Tariff of 1913 and raised rates to an average of 38 percent.

The nation was experiencing high levels of continued immigration, and so Harding signed the Emergency Quota Act of 1921. This law established the first general limits on immigration in the nation's history.

The waves of immigration from Europe that took place before World War I were the largest ever. Factory owners enjoyed the cheap labor the new immigrants provided, but many Americans feared that poor Europeans would bring with them dangerous ideas of communism. The Emergency Quota Act limited immigration from each country to 3 percent of the number of people from that country already in the United States in 1910.

Harding was ahead of his time when it came to African-American civil rights. He became the first president since the Civil War to deliver a speech in the South on behalf of equal rights for blacks. He was even more successful when it came to foreign affairs. The victorious nations of World War I were competing for power, Harding convened an international conference on arms control. The meeting ended with the U.S., Great Britain, France, Japan, and Italy all agreeing to limit the size of their navies. The U.S. and Great Britain were granted the largest fleets, with the Japanese fleet capped at slightly more than half of their size. The Italian and French navies were limited to a little more than half the size of the Japanese fleet.

The meeting also led to the Four Power Pact, including the U.S., Great Britain, Japan, and France. With this treaty, the four nations agreed to respect each other's territory in Asia. They also promised to resolve peacefully any disagreements among them.

Harding often employed his friends in political positions, even if they were not qualified. This would doom his presidency in what was called the Teapot Dome scandal. Rumors of corruption in his administration began circulating widely, and a formal investigation was opened. It was discovered that most of the people he had appointed to office were not qualified to be there. It appeared they were more interested in private gain than public service. The investigation proved that most of Harding's friends that had been appointed to office were crooks.

No one can be sure just how much Harding knew about what his friends were doing, but it was speculated that he had some knowledge of their corruption. In August of 1923, he suddenly became ill, and a few days later, he died. Then the stories began to surface. The worst of which involved the secretary of the interior who had rented publicly owned oil fields to private companies in exchange for over three million dollars in bribes. For this, he was sent to prison. Soon others were caught and either sent to prison or committed suicide before going to trial. As the people learned about how crooked Harding's administration had been, they began to wonder about the president's sudden illness and death. Rumors circulated that he had killed himself and others said that his wife poisoned him. The exact truth was never known, but now it seems probable that he died of a heart attack.

CALVIN COOLIDGE

30TH PRESIDENT: 1923 - 1929

Calvin Coolidge spent his childhood in Plymouth, Vermont, where his father was a shopkeeper and was active in politics. He graduated from Amherst College and practiced law in Northampton, Massachusetts. When he went into politics, he was elected to the state legislature. He became mayor of Northampton, then was elected lieutenant governor, and then governor.

He was not a typical politician. He had a lean and unpleasant look. When he made speeches, he kept them as short as possible. He became known as Silent Cal. He first drew national attention while he was governor of Massachusetts. In 1919, the police in Boston went on strike, and Coolidge promptly called out the entire National guard and broke the strike. Largely because of this action, he was nominated by the Republicans for vice president in 1920. When Harding died suddenly in 1923, Coolidge was awakened by a messenger in the middle of the night and informed that he was now the 30th President of the United States.

He was visiting his father at the time. By the light of a kerosene lamp, his hand on the old family Bible, Coolidge took the oath of office from his father, who was a justice of the peace. The scandals of the Harding administration were not yet public. Still, when they did become known, they did not bother Coolidge much. Even the Democrats never suspected Coolidge of being dishonest.

Coolidge had a large task of restoring the faith in the government and in the Republican party. He succeeded beyond anyone's expectations. His quiet style of leadership became his greatest asset. He moved aggressively to root out corruption, and by remaining calm, he soon persuaded Americans that the government's problems were over. He became a celebrated symbol of integrity in office.

Coolidge put an emphasis on the American business community. He often said, "The chief business of America is business." Almost everything he did was designed to benefit business. In his inaugural address, he proposed tax cuts. He argued that reducing the income tax burden on the wealthiest Americans would benefit everybody by increasing business activity. His new tax laws were very favorable to business. They lowered income taxes and eliminated other taxes that had been put in place to raise money for World War I. A majority of the prosperity of the 1920s resulted from these tax reforms.

As Coolidge had predicted, the tax cuts encouraged wealthy people to invest more of their money in business. What he did not anticipate is that so many people would take foolish risks in the hope of receiving higher returns. This unrestrained speculation was later seen as the cause of the 1929 stock market crash.

One of his most successful initiatives was his promotion of commercial aviation in the U.S. The aviation industry had grown at a rapid pace, and now passenger aircraft were becoming available for the very first time. In May of 1926, Congress passed the Air Commerce Act, which placed commercial aviation under government regulation so that the industry could be nurtured along. It also approved the first two commercial airline routes, one north and south, and the other east and west.

He also defeated bills in Congress that he thought unnecessary. One of which was the McNary-Haugen farm bill that stated that the government would have been required to buy surplus crops from U.S. farmers at a fixed price and then sell them abroad, often at a loss. The purpose was to protect farmers from unstable crop prices, but Coolidge thought it went against free-market economics. He argued that the government had no business fixing crop prices and that American farmers would make do with the laws of supply and demand. He believed crops should cost what people were willing to pay for them. At the time, these vetoes seemed sensible, but little did they know that down the road, they would significantly contribute to the suffering of farmers in the country and played a role in the Great Depression.

Coolidge most likely could have been elected again in 1928, but he decided against it, briefly stating, "I do not choose to run." He retired at the end of his term. This was lucky for Coolidge because a few months after the economic boom, the country plunged into the most terrible depression of its history. Millions of people lost their jobs, homes, and savings. Many committed suicide because they were ruined financially. He left politics and retired to write his autobiography, which was naturally a very short book.

HERBERT HOOVER
31ST PRESIDENT: 1929 - 1933

Herbert Hoover was the first President born west of the Mississippi River, in the town of West Branch, Iowa. His father was a blacksmith, but he died when Herbert was six years old. His mother, a deeply religious Quaker, supported her three children by preaching and taking in sewing commissions. She died when Herbert was nine, and so he moved to live with his uncle in Oregon. His uncle had a real estate office where Herbert worked after school. When he was seventeen, he went to Stanford University to study engineering. After he graduated, Hoover worked in San Francisco. When he was twenty-three, he went to Australia and helped develop one of the richest gold mines in the world. Two years later, he moved back to California and married his college sweetheart, Lou Henry. By his early thirties, Herbert was very wealthy.

Hoover was in England when World War I began. Suddenly many Americans who had been traveling abroad could not get money to go home. Hoover formed an organization that helped more than a hundred thousand Americans return from Europe. Much of the money he paid out of his own pocket. When the German army captured Belgium, many of the Belgian people were without food. Hoover helped bring food from the United States and get it through the German lines. His work saved millions of people from starving.

When America entered the war, President Wilson appointed Hoover the food administrator. His job was to get the American people to save food so it could be sent to the Allies and soldiers. Hoover had no real power to enforce his rules, but he was successful in his efforts. Due to his work, President Harding appointed Hoover secretary of commerce.

In 1928, the Republicans nominated Hoover for president. He had never run for any political office before, but most Americans knew him already and honored the work he had done. He was elected by a huge majority and became the 31st President of the United States.

Being a self-made millionaire, he seemed to be the right president for the times, which was in the middle of a boom. Then came the stock market crash, which changed everything. Hoover quickly met with business leaders and delivered speeches designed to restore confidence in the economy. His efforts were appreciated but weren't nearly enough to reverse the rapid decline of the economy.

The crash bankrupted investors who had been borrowing money to invest in the stock market. Its effects reached all Americans, whether they owned stocks or not. Over five thousand banks went bankrupt, wiping out the savings of nine million people. Over the next three years, an average of one hundred thousand people a week lost their jobs.

People who were scared of losing their jobs or had already lost them stopped making unnecessary purchases. As a result, businesses suffered more, and in turn, demand fell, so more jobs were lost. As people's savings ran out, they became unable to repay their debts, and many lost their homes. Farmers couldn't make a living due to crop prices being so low. By 1930, four million people were unemployed. By 1932, twelve million people were out of work. One in four Americans did not have a job. At its worst, starving people would line up for free soup and bread in towns and cities across the nation.

Congress responded by passing the Smoot-Hawley Tariff, which raised rates to record levels. Hoover knew that the bill was risky, but he went along anyway, thinking he had no other option. The goal was to increase sales of U.S. products by raising the cost of imported goods. This led to an international trade war as other nations raised their tariffs as well. This cut the sales of U.S. goods overseas and deepened the depression even more.

People wanted the government to give them aid in order to assist. Hoover was against this and was committed to individual responsibility. He worried that direct aid to people would make them dependent on the government and undermine their ability to make a living on their own.

Many people started to blame Hoover for their suffering. Homeless families that were living in shacks made out of cardboard called their shantytowns Hoovervilles. The newspapers they used to cover themselves were called Hoover blankets.

Throughout his term, Hoover refused to allow direct aid to the unemployed. He did, however, propose the creation of the Reconstruction Finance Corporation, which loaned two billion dollars to businesses, banks, and state government to help them survive the Great Depression. He believed the money would eventually trickle down to the people who needed it. While well-intended, it was too little too late.

After his presidency, he went back to private life. He was hated by many who thought he was to blame for the Great Depression. Gradually people understood that no one person was entirely to blame. Then in 1940, the Soviet Union and Finland went to war. Hoover raised great stocks of food to help feed the Finns. After World War II, President Truman named him as the head of the Famine Emergency Commission. This sent food to people in countries destroyed by war. Once more, Hoover's work helped save millions of lives.

FRANKLIN D. ROOSEVELT

32ND PRESIDENT: 1933 - 1945

Franklin Roosevelt was born into a wealthy and well-known family. President Theodore Roosevelt was his fifth cousin. Franklin was also distantly related to ten other presidents: Washington, both Adamses, Madison, Van Buren, both Harrisons, Taylor, Grant, and Taft.

As a boy, he never went to public schools. An only child, he traveled with his parents in Europe. He learned foreign languages from his private tutors. When he was fourteen, he was sent to Groton, a private school. He later attended Harvard and became editor of the school paper his senior year. He went on to study law. He married a distant cousin named Eleanor Roosevelt. Eleanor's father was dead, so at the wedding, Franklin's cousin, President Teddy Roosevelt, gave the bride away.

Franklin greatly admired his cousin Teddy. He, too, believed that politics offered a wealthy man a chance to serve his country. Unlike Teddy, Franklin followed in his father's footsteps and was a Democrat. He began his career by running for the New York State Legislature, to which he was elected. He was then appointed assistant secretary of the Navy by President Wilson, which was a post his cousin Teddy Roosevelt once held. When World War I started, he wanted to quit his job and join the Navy. Wilson would not let him go and told him that his work was too important.

After the war, Roosevelt was nominated by the Democrats to run for vice president. This gave him a chance to meet people all around the country. Then, in 1921, he became ill with polio, and for a time, he couldn't move his arms or legs. Slowly, he fought his way back and regained the use of his hand and arms. He spent long hours swimming and exercising. He was never able to walk again without braces on his legs and crutches.

He was elected Governor of New York in 1928. This was during the Great Depression. As Governor,

Roosevelt used the power of the state to help businesses and people who were out of work. He talked to the people over the radio. He called these talks 'fireside chats,' and in them, he told people what he was trying to do.

The Democrats nominated Roosevelt for President in 1932. He ran against Herbert Hoover who was extremely unpopular at the time. He won the election and became the 32nd President of the United States.

Similar to Abraham Lincoln, Roosevelt became president during a time of great national crisis. Banks were closing around the country and industrial production had been cut in half. More than thirteen million people had been put out of work, and one-quarter of the nation's farmers had lost their lands.

Roosevelt knew quick action was needed. He tried to reassure the people stating, "the only thing we have to fear is fear itself." His cabinet appointments showed that he intended to make drastic changes in the way the government was run.

The first issue for Roosevelt to take on was the banking crisis. Since so many banks had gone under, the American people were losing faith in the country's financial institutions. People began lining up at the banks to take out their money rather than lose it. These runs on the bank threatened the entire system. Roosevelt immediately declared a national bank holiday, halting all banking operations in the United States. Three days after that, Congress passed the Emergency Banking Act, which endorsed the president's action and kept the banks closed until federal auditors could review the books.

During his first 'fireside chat,' he explained to the public the government's new banking policy, which restored much of their faith in the system. Within a few weeks, more than twelve thousand banks with 90 percent of the nation's deposits had reopened. This also halted runs on the banks.

He followed this up with aggressive banking reform. He signed the Banking Act, which created the Federal Deposit Insurance Corporation, which guaranteed individual accounts of up to five thousand dollars. This gave depositors confidence that even if a bank went under, they would not lose their money.

There was also a crisis in agriculture that needed to be resolved. Even before the Great Depression, farmers had been suffering from low crop prices, which drastically fell after the stock market crash.

The Agricultural Adjustment Act of May 1933 attempted to raise crop prices by cutting farm production. It authorized the government to pay farmers for taking land out of cultivation. This seemed a cruel thing to do while millions of Americans were starving in the cities, but the government argued that farmers could not make a living any other way.

Of all of the New Deal programs Roosevelt put into place, the cornerstone was the National Industrial Recovery Act of 1933. This law established the National Recovery Administration, which worked with business groups to create "codes of fair competition" for their industries. It was believed that these codes would provide a basis for regulating the marketplace. Roosevelt suspended the nation's antitrust laws so that prices and production quotas could be fixed. In exchange, he demanded a number of concessions for workers, including higher wages.

One of the most lasting innovations Roosevelt implemented was the Social Security Act of 1935. This law provided for payments to people who were old, unemployed, sick, or disabled. At about the same time, Congress also passed the National Labor Relations Act, which made it illegal for employers to interfere with union organizing, and the Revenue Act of 1935 raised individual income tax rates as high as 75 percent for people earning more than five million dollars a year.

By the time Roosevelt began his second term in 1937, government spending had brought about a limited recovery. The president was frustrated by his unfinished success, and he was also upset with the Supreme Court for blocking some of his more unorthodox initiatives. Roosevelt wanted to reorganize the Supreme Court and to appoint a new justice for each justice currently over seventy years of age. More than six of the justices were already older than seventy, enactment of this plan would have allowed Roosevelt to appoint six additional justices, bringing the total number to fifteen. While most agreed there should be some reform, few agreed with his plan. The Senate eventually rejected the plan, but during that time, the justices got the message he was trying to send them. They stopped blocking his attempts at more New Deal legislation.

During the Summer of 1940, Roosevelt had kept his reelection plans a secret. Not even the delegates to the Democratic convention knew what he intended to do. Roosevelt was working behind the scenes to have the convention draft him. Never before had a president run for a third term, and Roosevelt was worried that the voters might think him arrogant. By having the convention draft him, Roosevelt's plan was to pretend that a third term had been forced on him by the will of the people. Since there was so much going on internationally at the time, the country decided to stick with their proven leader and elected Roosevelt to a third term.

World War II began in September of 1939 when Nazi Germany invaded Poland. This caused Britain and France, which were allies of Poland, to declare war on Germany. Roosevelt had promised to be a 'good neighbor' and not get involved in foreign affairs, so he was reluctant to go back on his word and join the fight. Roosevelt saw the threat that Hitler posed, and after the fall of France in 1940, he did all he could within the law to save the British. In September, he sent fifty surplus destroyers to Great Britain in exchange for the use of naval bases in Newfoundland and Bermuda. The British desperately needed these destroyers to fight the German U-boats. Roosevelt thought he could do more, so he proposed the Lend-Lease Act, which meant arms could be sent immediately to Britain, but payments deferred until after the war.

In August of 1941, Roosevelt met with British prime minister Winston Churchill. This marked the beginning of a very close relationship between the two men. They drew up the Atlantic Charter, which defined their common war aims. Most importantly, among these was the right of every people to choose their own form of government.

The United States finally entered World War II when the Japanese bombed Pearl Harbor in December of 1941. Tensions between the two countries had been building since Japan joined the axis powers of Germany and Italy and signed a pact that stated war against one meant war against all. Roosevelt quickly shifted the country's economy in order to prepare for the war. Nearly every person and resource in the country was playing some part in the war effort.

General Dwight D Eisenhower, the top Allied commander in Europe, decided that the invasion of France would take place in Normandy on June 6, 1944. This was code-named D-day. The success of this invasion gave the Allies a foothold in Europe, which they kept expanding until France was liberated.

Success was growing, and the end of the war was in sight. At that time, Roosevelt's health was also on the decline. Roosevelt met with Churchill and Joseph Stalin (Soviet Union Premier) to discuss plans for post-war. Stalin forced the president to agree to the creation of Communist governments in Eastern Europe. Many historians claim that it was Roosevelt's poor health, which is to blame for why he agreed to the concessions.

On April 12, 1945, as the Allies converged on Berlin, Roosevelt died. He was resting at his cottage in Warm Spring, Georgia, while an artist was painting his picture. All of a sudden, he put a hand to his head and fell backward in his chair. A few hours later, he was pronounced dead. All over the world, people mourned his death. In Europe, on ships at sea, in the jungles of the South Pacific, soldiers and sailors wept openly. As one sailor said, "It's tough when one of your buddies has to go, and President Roosevelt was our buddy." Less than a month later, on May 7th, the Germans formally surrendered, ending the war in Europe.

HARRY S. TRUMAN
33RD PRESIDENT: 1945 - 1953

As a child, Harry Truman was often sick. By the time he was eight, he had to wear thick glasses. Since they were so expensive, he wasn't allowed to play contact sports with the rest of his friends. He was often teased for this, having to take piano lessons rather than playing outdoors. Before he was fourteen, he said he had read every book in the library in Independence, Missouri. He did not attend college, he worked for a railroad, at a bank, and on the family farm. He was thirty-three when World War I began, and he promptly volunteered and went to France as a captain of artillery. When he returned home, he married his high school sweetheart and started a men's clothing store. The store failed, and Truman decided to go into politics.

With the help of a local political boss named Tom Pendergast, he was elected to be the county judge. In 1934, also with help from Pendergast, he won a seat in the United States Senate. Although Pendergast was corrupt and later sent to prison for cheating on his income taxes and fixing elections, Truman was regarded as an honest public servant.

When Roosevelt ran for his fourth term in 1944, he requested that Truman be nominated for vice president. After being elected, Roosevelt gave Truman very little to do and did not keep him up to date with what was going on. Suddenly Roosevelt died, and Truman became the 33rd President of the United States. Roosevelt had been running the country for twelve years, so it was quite a task to replace him, especially during a time of war. Roosevelt had brought the country through the Great Depression and won World War II in Europe, but Japan still had to be defeated, and communism already seemed to be a growing threat as well.

Since Truman had not been kept up to date on what Roosevelt was doing, he was at an even greater disadvantage when taking over his office. Truman wasn't even briefed on the atomic bomb project until after he became president. As a result, he had to learn many things in a very short amount of time. His first important test came in July of 1945 when he traveled to Germany to meet with British prime minister Winston Churchill and Soviet Premier Joseph Stalin to decide what to do with postwar Germany.

The day before the meeting, American scientists conducted the first atomic bomb test in New Mexico. The British were aware of the test because they had helped with the research, but the Soviets had been told nothing of the Manhattan Project. After learning of the test's success, Truman decided to tell Stalin about the new U.S. super weapon.

Ten days later, the Allied leadership decided to send an ultimatum to the Japanese, "The alternative to surrender is prompt and utter destruction." The Japanese were not aware of the atomic bomb, so they saw no reason to surrender.

Their defiance compelled Truman to make one of the most terrifying decisions ever forced on a president. He had to decide whether or not to use the atomic bomb on a city. If he used the bomb, hundreds of thousands of Japanese civilians would die, but if he didn't, hundreds of thousands of American soldiers might also die. Truman decided that his primary responsibility was to safeguard the lives of U.S. servicemen. Truman gave the orders to drop the bomb on two Japanese cities, Hiroshima and Nagasaki. Four days later, Japan surrendered. As one war ended, another war began.

Stalin made it clear that he would accept nothing less than secure postwar borders for the Soviet Union. He wanted a clear Soviet-dominated communist government in Eastern Europe. Stalin feared that the Germans would recover quickly, as they had after World War I, and he wanted a buffer zone. Truman and Churchill feared the Germans much less than the Soviets, and they were particularly concerned about Stalin's imposition of communism in Eastern Europe. In a speech delivered in Missouri, Churchill declared that an "iron curtain" was falling across Europe. On one side were the democrats of the West, and on the other side were the communists of the East. This struggle became known as the Cold War. Although the U.S. and Soviets never fought each other directly, they did so through the Koreans and the Vietnamese.

The first major conflict of the Cold War took place in the Mediterranean, where communist rebels threatened to overthrow elected governments in Greece and Turkey. Truman wanted to check the spread of communism, so he requested four-hundred-million dollars in aid to the two countries. He argued that the United States must help every nation facing a communist threat. This policy later became known as the Truman Doctrine.

Secretary of State George C Marshall began working on the rebuilding of war-ravaged Europe. Nearly six years of tank battles and Allied bombing had reduced its industrial cities to rubble. It was determined that the only way to save the rebuilding nations of Western Europe from communism was to get their economies rolling again. Between 1948 and 1952, Congress appropriated thirteen billion dollars for this plan. Half of this money went to Britain, France, and West Germany. Soon the Soviet Union decided to test the West's resolve in Berlin. In order to get the British, French, and Americans to leave, the Soviets decided to blockade West Berlin. Truman quickly ordered the airlifting of goods to the city by using shuttles of cargo planes. The United States and Great Britain were able to keep West Berlin supplied with food, coal, and other necessities. The blockade ended a month later when the Soviets reopened the roads leading in and out of the city. The Berlin airlift made clear the need for a united front in Western Europe, which led to the North Atlantic Treaty Organization, otherwise known as NATO.

Of all the nations that fought in World War II, only the United States came out of it better off economically. After years of rationing, Americans were eager to spend the money they had saved on large purchases such as cars and houses.

At the end of the war, there were 12 million men and women serving in the armed forces. Within a year, 9 million would be discharged. Truman worried that the discharged soldiers would have a difficult time finding new jobs now that many of their old jobs had been taken over by women and blacks. Two new trends did ease the job crunch. One was women began leaving the workforce to become housewives and mothers. The other was the nation's postwar spending spree created new jobs in manufacturing and homebuilding.

After his surprise reelection, Truman reintroduced his Fair Deal programs to a receptive Democratic Congress. He succeeded in raising the minimum wage from forty to seventy-five cents an hour and won passage of the National Housing Act, which funded slum clearance and low-income housing.

China was "lost" to communism in 1949, and this hurt the Truman administration. People debated who was at fault. During this debate, communist North Korea invaded anti-communist South Korea. Truman quickly sent U.S. troops to assist, and although the North Koreans had penetrated deeply into South Korea, the U.S. troops were able to turn the war around. General Douglas MacArthur was the leader of the United Nations (UN) forces at the time. He commanded the forces and crossed the border into North Korea and quickly advanced on the border between China and North Korea. As MacArthur approached, Chinese officials warned the United States they would not sit by and do nothing. MacArthur dismissed these warnings and assumed he would easily be able to handle anything they threw at him. He was wrong, and Chinese soldiers streamed across the river, inflicting heavy casualties and chasing the UN forces all the way back across the South Korean border.

He asked Truman for permission to carry the war into China, and Truman refused. MacArthur took his case to the public which was more than any commander in chief could tolerate, and so Truman relieved MacArthur of his command. Three months later, peace talks began, but no treaty was signed while Truman was in office.

DWIGHT D. EISENHOWER

34TH PRESIDENT: 1953 - 1961

*D*wight Eisenhower grew up in Kansas as the third of six sons born into a poor family. He was often teased for wearing tattered clothing and his mother's old shoes. He had his heart set on going to the Naval Academy in Annapolis. He wanted to be a sailor, but the examination he took to enter Annapolis was the same required for the army school at West Point. On his paper, he had to mark one of three choices: army, navy, or either.

Eisenhower marked the word 'either,' and it was decided that he would attend West Point. While there, he played football until he injured his knee. During World War I, Eisenhower was a training officer in the U.S. When World War II began, he was asked to draw up plans for war in the Pacific. These were so good that President Roosevelt promoted him over 366 other officers to head the U.S. armies in Europe. Soon he was made commander of all the Allied Forces.

This job required much more than just military skills. He was required to get along with generals from a half dozen countries. He also had to get along with politicians who headed these countries. It was his skill and personal charm that made him so successful in this job.

After the war, he retired from the army and was appointed president of Columbia University. In 1948, both political parties wanted him to run for president. He refused and said he did not believe a professional military man should be president. They kept after him, and in 1952, he agreed to join the Republican ticket. While he was not a good public speaker and would fumble over his words, it was clear that he was an honest man. He had a large grin that made people feel they knew him personally, and everyone liked him. He won an easy victory, becoming the 34th President of the United States and the first Republican president in twenty years.

Eisenhower believed the government should remain as small as possible. He was a moderate who fell straight down the middle.

In December of 1952, he kept his campaign promise and traveled to Korea, where he tried to revive the stalled Korean War peace talks. He threatened to take the war into China and also said he was open to using atomic weapons if needed. The talks dragged on for another seven months before an armistice was signed. By the time the war in Korea ended, the United States had spent fifty billion dollars. To avoid paying such a high price in the future, Eisenhower developed the policy of "massive retaliation." In their view, the Soviet Union would not attack the U.S. or any of its allies, as long as the leaders in the Kremlin believed that the U.S. would respond with nuclear devastation.

Because nuclear weapons offered so much power and "more bang for a buck" than conventional weapons, Eisenhower ordered severe cutbacks in army ground troops and instead invested in nuclear warheads. He also spent money on the aircraft needed to deliver these weapons. The costs began to increase instead of decrease as new technology was needed.

The country became obsessed with communists that were living in the U.S. According to Eisenhower's cabinet communists were everywhere: in factories, offices, butcher shops and on street corners. Wisconsin Senator Joseph McCarthy quickly became famous for his crusade against communists in the State Department, which he claimed was full of them. McCarthy cleverly spoke in half-truths and insinuations that could be neither proved nor disproved. Although he never proved any of these outrageous accusations, Eisenhower and others in a position of power refrained from criticizing him because they feared his wrath. Many also believe that attacking McCarthy would make them look suspicious. People that were accused by McCarthy, many of which were writers and actors, were often prevented from working. The practice of blacklisting people that were feared to be communists ruined the careers of many innocent people.

McCarthy's arrogance finally caught up with him in 1954 when he chaired a series of nationally televised hearings related to alleged communists in the armed forces. A lawyer for the army named Joseph Welch finally challenged the senator publicly after McCarthy tried to smear one of Welch's young legal assistants. Welch's public chastising of McCarthy broke his power over Washington, and in December, the Senate voted to reprimand McCarthy for "conduct unbecoming a member."

The Supreme Court grabbed headlines when Eisenhower named California governor Earl Warren to be the new chief justice. Eisenhower thought he was making an uncontroversial, middle-of-the-road appointment, but instead, Warren led a revolution on the Court, particularly in regards to civil rights law.

In May of 1954, the court unanimously reversed *Plessy v. Ferguson*, the 1896 case that had upheld the legality of 'separate but equal' treatment for blacks. In deciding *Brown vs. Board of Education*, Warren wrote that segregating white and black students in public schools was unequal and, therefore, unconstitutional. Later, Eisenhower said that appointing Warren was "the biggest damn fool mistake I ever made."

The civil rights movement gained great momentum during the Eisenhower administration. Martin Luther King Jr. rose from Alabama to become the movement's most eloquent spokesperson. Dr. King led the Montgomery bus boycott, which brought together the black community and drew national attention to the fight for equal rights.

Eisenhower objected to racial segregation, but he also believed that trying to force integration on the South would be politically foolish. When he finally sent troops into Little Rock to ensure the admission of black students into Central High School, he did so only because the Arkansas governor was challenging federal authority, not because he believed that integrating public schools was the right thing to do.

With the public's attention so closely focused on what was going on in Little Rock, it came as a shock to most Americans when the Soviet Union announced the successful launch of *Sputnik*, the first human-made object ever placed in orbit around the earth. Congress was upset because the Soviet Union had beaten the United States into space, which led them to pass the National Defense Education Act. Its goal was to develop new scientific talent through the funding of school laboratory construction and college scholarships for promising students. The students would have to swear a loyalty oath, saying they were not sympathetic to communism before they were allowed to receive any scholarship funds.

This kicked off the "space race" between the two nations.

In an attempt to ease the tensions of the Cold War, Eisenhower and Soviet Premier Nikita Khrushchev agreed to meet in a series of cultural exchanges. In July of 1959, Vice President Richard Nixon visited Moscow to open a U.S. exhibition there. He crossed paths with Khrushchev at a kitchen display, and the two engaged in a loud, spontaneous debate as to whether communism or capitalism was better. The press called this the Kitchen Debate. Two months later, Khrushchev made a goodwill visit to the U.S. and had positive conversations with Eisenhower. The two leaders met at Camp David, the presidential retreat named after Eisenhower's grandson. They agreed to continue working together in "the spirit of Camp David" and made plans for a meeting in Paris the following May.

Less than two weeks before the Paris summit, the Soviet Union shot down a U.S. spy plane deep within Soviet airspace. At first, the State Department issued denials, but Eisenhower later admitted that U-2 planes had been making secret high-altitude flights over Soviet territory for years. He ended the flights, but he refused to apologize for them. Khrushchev canceled the Paris summit.

At the end of his second term, Eisenhower was seventy years old, the oldest man to ever be President. He was happy to retire to a farm he had bought near Gettysburg, Pennsylvania. Since he had spent so much time in the army, it was the first home he and his wife had ever owned. He lived there until his death in 1969.

JOHN F. KENNEDY
35TH PRESIDENT: 1961 - 1963

*J*ohn Kennedy's father, Joseph Kennedy, was a businessman who made a large fortune. He was the second oldest of nine children, and Joseph gave each of them a million dollars when they became twenty-one. As a child, John looked up to his older brother Joe, whom their father predicted would one day become president. John went to study at Harvard. When World War II began, John joined the Navy. He was the skipper of a PT boat in the South Pacific. During a night battle, a Japanese destroyer rammed into his small boat, cutting it into two. Two men were killed, and Kennedy's back was badly hurt. Despite his injury, Kennedy swam for hours, towing another man who was injured even worse than John. John's older brother Joe, who his father had predicted would go into politics, was killed during the war. So the family decided that John would take his place. He ran for Congress, and the whole family pitched in to help. His brothers and sisters made speeches as well as thousands of phone calls.

Kennedy was elected and served three terms in the house of representatives before he was elected to the Senate.

His back injury still bothered him, and so he decided to have an operation. While he was recovering, he wrote a book called *Profiles in Courage* about United States senators who had risked their careers to fight for things they believed in. It won a prize for the best American history book of that year.

Kennedy, with the help of his family, decided to run for president. In 1956 he tried for the Democratic vice-presidential nomination but lost. He immediately started working toward the next election with his family. Since they were all wealthy, money was no issue, so they traveled back and forth across the country, making speeches and talking with politicians. When the Democratic Convention met, he was nominated for president on the first ballot.

Kennedy was only forty-three years old, and so many thought he was too young. They did not think he had enough experience. For the first time during a presidential campaign, the candidates, Kennedy, and Richard Nixon debated with each other on television. This was a big help to Kennedy as he was not only handsome but was also charming. The election was very close, but Kennedy won and became the 35th President of the United States.

Kennedy might be best known for the hope he gave the nation. In 1961, the nation was dealing with the Cold War abroad and racial injustices at home. In his inaugural address, Kennedy admitted these problems but also spoke optimistically of a new generation of Americans ready to solve them.

In one of the most quoted speeches ever, Kennedy spoke of the goals and promised to work for freedom around the world but also asked Americans to give something of themselves. "Ask not what your country can do for you. Ask what you can do for your country."

When Eisenhower left office, he told Kennedy that the Central Intelligence Agency was secretly training Cuban exiles to overthrow Fidel Castro. Since Castro's successful revolution, Cuba had become increasingly friendly with the Soviet Union. Having a Soviet ally so close to the United States shore made the president nervous, so Kennedy allowed the secret training to continue.

On April 17th, 1961, fourteen hundred Cuban exiles landed at the Bay of Pigs. Their mission was to lead a popular revolt against Castro. Few Cubans joined them, and the U.S. air support never arrived to assist. As a result, the invasion was a disaster, and President Kennedy was forced to take the blame at the very beginning of his administration.

Later in August, the Soviet-backed government of East Germany built a wall separating East Berlin from West Berlin. The U.S. protested, but because the wall was built entirely on the East Berlin side, it was allowed to stand.

Kennedy had another serious encounter with the Soviet Union in October of 1962 when he discovered that the Soviets were building nuclear missile bases in Cuba. The president ordered Navy ships to surround the island. After a standoff, Soviet Premier Nikita Khrushchev agreed to remove the missiles in exchange for a U.S. promise not to invade Cuba. The Cuban Missile Crisis was the closest the world has ever come to nuclear war.

Kennedy reluctantly heeded the black community's growing demand for civil rights. Although he personally favored equal rights for all, he wanted to move slowly so as not to offend segregationist Democrats in the South. Activists like Martin Luther King Jr. were tired of waiting, and they forced Kennedy to act. In 1961, thirteen black and white Freedom Riders boarded a Greyhound bus in Washington, D.C. headed for the Deep South. Their purpose was to protest racial segregation in public transport. At nearly every stop, they were attacked and beaten. Since what they were doing was legal, Kennedy was eventually forced to protect them.

In a speech made soon after his inauguration, Kennedy vowed that the United States would land a man on the moon by the end of the decade. To achieve this goal, he launched a five-billion-dollar space program. Space was yet another arena in which the United States and the Soviet Union were in direct competition. This drew the country together and led to optimism about our future, inspired by Kennedy.

Kennedy also created the Peace Corps in 1961 so that Americans could help the people of developing countries in a more direct capacity. Doctors, teachers, scientists, and other volunteers built hospitals, started schools, and improved farming methods all over the world and many recent graduates were inspired to join the Peace Corps.

On November 22, 1963, about one thousand days into his presidency, Kennedy flew to Dallas to deliver a speech. He and his wife Jackie were greeted by huge cheering crowds all the way from the airport. As their convertible entered Dealey Plaza, a number of shots were fired at Kennedy from a nearby building. Two hit the president, one in the throat and the other in the back of the head. Kennedy died at a nearby hospital about a half-hour later. The entire nation was in shock because he was so young and vital, the people mourned him as they had mourned no president since Lincoln.

LYNDON B. JOHNSON
36TH PRESIDENT: 1963 - 1969

Lyndon Johnson's father and grandfather had both been members of the Texas Legislature. The day Lyndon was born, his grandfather mounted his horse and went galloping around the country, saying, "A United States Senator has just been born!"

His parents taught him to read by the time he was four. In school, he got excellent grades, but when he finished high school, he thought he had enough education. He traveled around the country, working at odd jobs until he finally went back home, claiming that he was sick of working with his hands. He went to college and became interested in campus politics. He organized a political party that won all the campus elections.

After college, Johnson taught school. He could not leave politics, so he started working for a man named Robert Kleberg, who was running for Congress. Kleberg was elected and took Johnson to Washington as his secretary.

Working for Kleberg required Johnson to travel back and forth to Texas. On one of these trips, he met Claudia Taylor, and within a few months, they were married. When he was twenty-nine years old, he ran for Congress and was elected. A few years later, when the Japanese bombed Pearl Harbor, Johnson quickly asked for active duty in the Navy and became the first member of Congress to go into uniform.

After World War II, Johnson was elected to the U.S. Senate. He proved to be one of the best senators in history as he had a great gift for getting people with different ideas to work together. In 1960, Johnson was elected vice president under Kennedy. When Kennedy was killed, Johnson became the 36th President of the United States. He promised the American people to carry on with Kennedy's plans.

The country was still in shock over the assassination of Kennedy, but Johnson knew that there was work to be done. Johnson was a shrewd politician who knew how to get things done. He persuaded Congress to approve ten new anti-poverty programs with total funding of one billion dollars. These included the Job Corps for disadvantaged teenagers and Head Start for preschool children.

To assist blacks, he pushed through the Civil Rights Act of 1964, which made it illegal for employers to discriminate on the basis of race. It also outlawed segregation in public places such as hotels and restaurants.

Of all the laws passed during his presidency, he was most proud of the Voting Rights Act of 1965. This outlawed literacy tests and other unfair practices used to keep blacks from registering to vote. The new law made huge voter registration drives possible, and with more blacks registered, black candidates won more elections. A year later, President Johnson nominated Thurgood Marshall to the Supreme Court.

After Johnson's victory in the 1964 election, the Great Society became the theme of his domestic program. He developed Medicaid and Medicare to help poor people and the elderly pay their medical bills. He also put in place the first significant environmental and consumer laws, which set standards for air and water quality as well as auto safety.

The Vietnam War was starting to become costly, and as the fighting escalated, Johnson asked an increasingly reluctant Congress for more funds. In early August of 1964, the president announced that the US ship *Maddox* had been attacked by North Vietnamese patrol boats in international waters while on patrol. The president immediately sent Congress a resolution granting him nearly unlimited authority to use U.S. military force in Vietnam. It passed unanimously in the House and mostly in the Senate as well. Initially, only thirty-five hundred marines would land at Da Nang, but within two years, there would be four hundred thousand more.

Johnson's military advisers kept telling him a victory was right around the corner. On January 30th, 1968, the North Vietnamese and their Vietcong allies launched a surprise attack on major cities in the South. The assault was called the Tet-Offensive because it began during a cease-fire to celebrate Tet, the Vietnamese New Year. Until the Tet-Offensive, it was possible for Americans to believe the U.S. might actually be winning the war, but after it was obvious that victory was a long way off or not even possible at all. As a result, many moderates joined the growing antiwar movement.

Because of the racial problems at home and the war in Vietnam, the people of the United States grew more divided. They grew angry at one another and at the president. At first, Johnson had been a popular president, but now he became one of the most disliked. He was especially criticized by young people. They staged huge demonstrations across the country to protest the war. They burned American flags and army draft cards. Johnson was deeply affected by these protests. On March 31, 1968, Johnson made a television speech that surprised the nation. He called for a temporary halt to the bombing of North Vietnam so that peace talks could begin. He also said, " I shall not seek, and I will not accept, the nomination of my party for another term as your president."

Johnson retired to his Texas ranch when his term was over in 1969. Four years later, he died of a heart attack.

RICHARD NIXON
37TH PRESIDENT: 1969 - 1974

*R*ichard Nixon was still a small boy when his parents moved to Whittier, California. His father ran a grocery store and a small filling station. Richard worked in both stores. He would often get up at four in the morning to go into the nearby city of Los Angeles to buy fresh vegetables for the grocery. Then he was back home and ready for school by eight o'clock.

Nixon was a good student and graduated from Whittier College and then won a scholarship to Duke University, where he went on to study law. He went back to California to practice until World War II started and he joined the Navy. After the war, he was asked to run for Congress on the Republican ticket in California. His district normally elected a Democrat, but he worked hard, and he won. He served two terms in the House of Representatives and then was elected to the Senate. In 1952, presidential candidate Dwight Eisenhower selected Nixon as his running mate as vice president. He spent most of his time as vice president traveling to fifty-six different countries representing the U.S. government. When Eisenhower got sick, Nixon served as acting president.

In 1960, Nixon ran for president against John F. Kennedy and was defeated in a very close election. He went back to California and ran for governor. He was again defeated, and he blamed the press for his loss. He told reporters, "You won't have Nixon to kick around anymore because, gentlemen, this is my last press conference." He vowed to never run for office again. Instead, he moved to New York and joined a law firm.

He continued to work with politicians and helped many of them who were running for office. They, in turn, helped him get nominated for president in 1968, and this time he won becoming the 37th President of the United States.

Nixon spoke of his secret plan to end the conflict in Vietnam while campaigning. It turns out his 'secret plan' was to replace U.S. combat troops with South Vietnamese soldiers. Kennedy and Johnson both thought this was a good idea at one time but then realized that the South Vietnamese were incapable of fighting their own war. Nixon went ahead with his plan because he had no other ideas. To make up for the resulting decline in combat strength, Nixon stepped up the bombing of North Vietnam. As a result, more American bomb tonnage was dropped on North Vietnam than on Germany, Italy, and Japan during all of World War II.

Meanwhile, as he tried to bring peace in Vietnam, Nixon worked on the greatest foreign policy initiative of his career. His whole life, he had fought communism, and his hostility towards communists was well known. That's why Nixon's 1971 announcement that he would visit the People's Republic of China stunned the world. The trip was arranged by Henry Kissinger and took place in February of 1972, which involved a meeting between Nixon and Mao Tse-Tung. This was the first step in restoring a diplomatic relationship.

Having opened the door to China, Nixon was now able to play on the strained relations between China and the Soviet Union. Although they were both run by communist governments, neither trusted the other, and Nixon hoped that by forging ties with China, he could weaken Soviet power and influence. Not long after his return from China, he followed up that success with another trip to Moscow. Nixon had visited Moscow once before in 1959 when he and Nikita Khrushchev had met in the Kitchen Debate. This trip was highlighted by the signing of a nuclear arms control treaty.

In October of 1972, just two weeks before the election, Henry Kissinger announced that peace was at hand in Vietnam. After the U.S. election, the agreement hit a snag when each side accused the other of bargaining in bad faith. To bring the North Vietnamese back to the table, Nixon ordered the heaviest bombing of the war. During the bombing, more than two hundred B-52s flew missions around the clock over North Vietnam. A formal peace agreement was finally signed in January 1973. The South Vietnamese government retained control of Saigon while the Vietcong remained in place in the countryside. The U.S. agreed to remove all of its combat troops within sixty days in return for the release of prisoners of war.

On June 17, 1972, police arrested five men caught breaking into the Democratic National Committee headquarters in Washington. One of the men arrested at the Watergate office building was James McCord, who was a former FBI agent now working for the committee to reelect the president. When asked about the break-in, President Nixon denied any knowledge, insisting that no one at the White House knew anything of the incident. The cover-up had just begun.

At first, the scandal seemed limited to Nixon's reelection committee until the *Washington Post* began writing stories that suggested the break-in had been part of a much larger dirty campaign. The two reporters, Woodward and Bernstein, allegations were confirmed by McCord in a letter he wrote to the federal district court judge who was hearing the Watergate burglary case. While asking for leniency, McCord admitted that officials had lied under oath. He named former attorney general John Mitchell as the boss. In February of 1973, the Senate created a special committee to look into any illegal or unethical activities that might have occurred during the 1972 campaign.

In July, presidential assistant Alexander Butterfield revealed in passing that President Nixon had been secretly recording Oval Office conversations. The Senate committee then subpoenaed the tapes. When Nixon refused to turn them over, arguing that executive privilege allowed him to keep the conversations private, the special prosecution brought it to the federal courts.

One factor that delayed his impeachment was the reality that if forced from office, he would be succeeded by Vice President Spiro T. Agnew, whom the Democrats despised even more than Nixon. Agnew was best known for his attacks on intellectuals and reporters. Most Democrats considered the prospect of an Agnew presidency horrifying. However, Agnew was forced to resign the vice presidency after pleading no contest to charges of accepting bribes while governor of Maryland. Two days later, Nixon nominated Gerald R Ford to replace him.

Meanwhile, the tapes case had reached the Court of Appeals, which ordered the president to turn them over. Throughout the winter and spring of 1974, subpoenas for White House tapes continued to be issued, and Nixon continued to fight them. He did release a few recordings and provided edited transcripts of others, but the committee kept pressing for the actual recording of the most sensitive conversations. Finally, the Supreme Court ruled unanimously that Nixon had to turn over all the tapes. Three days later, the Judiciary Committee approved the first of three articles of impeachment against him.

Historians have sometimes called Nixon paranoid, saying that he often thought people were out to get him. As proof, they point to the list of enemies that the president ordered his staff to keep. This list included not only political opponents but also journalists, athletes, movie stars, and businessmen. Names on the enemies list included Bill Cosby, Jane Fonda, and quarterback Joe Namath. Nixon ordered FBI Director J. Edgar Hoover to collect damaging information on some of these people using illegal wiretaps.

Nixon kept insisting that he was not a crook. These overturned tapes showed without a doubt that Nixon had taken part in a coverup. He had tried to keep the FBI from investigating and lied repeatedly.

The country was outraged, and to avoid impeachment, Nixon resigned his office on August 14, 1974. It was one of the most tragic moments in the history of the American presidency as never before had a president resigned.

GERALD R. FORD

38TH PRESIDENT: 1974 - 1977

Gerald Ford was born by the name Leslie Lynch King. He was named for his father; however, his parents were divorced soon after his birth, and his mother married a man named Gerald Rudolph Ford. Ford adopted his baby stepson, and the child's name was changed to Gerald R. Ford, Jr.

Gerald grew up in Grand Rapids, Michigan, enjoying sports like football, basketball, and track. His family had little money, so Gerald usually did odd jobs like mowing lawns and working in restaurants. His grades were good, and he was given a one-hundred-dollar scholarship to the University of Michigan. While the money helped, it did not pay all of his living expenses, so he waited tables on the side and worked as a janitor as well. He was also a member of Michigan's football team, where he played center. His senior year, he was named the team's MVP.

Ford wanted to attend law school, but money was an issue. He got a job as an assistant football coach at Yale, and in the offseason, he attended law classes. He graduated and went back to Grand Rapids to practice. But soon, World War II began, and Ford quit the law to join the Navy. He was assigned to the light aircraft carrier *Monterey* where he saw some of the fiercest battles of the war in the Pacific.

After the war, he returned to Grand Rapids and joined a large law firm. He also joined a number of civic organizations where he made many friends. He was asked to run for Congress as a Republican and was easily elected. He was reelected time after time and often with no opposition. His fellow congressmen liked and respected him. He served on important committees and helped investigate the murder of President Kennedy. In 1965, he was elected the leader of the Republican members of the House of Representatives.

He wanted to become the speaker of the House, but since the Republicans were the minority party, that made his dream difficult. He decided to run for Congress once more in 1974 and then retire in 1976. In 1973, Spiro Agnew, who was Nixon's vice president, was accused of taking bribes and resigned in disgrace. President Nixon asked Ford to become vice president, and Ford agreed, knowing he could still retire at the end of 1976 as planned.

President Nixon was caught in the Watergate scandal and forced to resign on August 14, 1974. Ford then became the 38th President of the United States and also became the first man to be president without ever having run for the office of either president or vice president.

Ford was sworn into office minutes after Richard Nixon's resignation took effect. Exactly one month after taking office, President Ford pardoned Richard Nixon for any crimes he might have committed while in office. It was Ford's opinion that the country needed to be spared the spectacle of a former president standing trial. This contributed to the low expectations that Americans had for him. People viewed Ford as more of a caretaker than as a leader.

The enormous cost of the Vietnam War had a lasting effect on the U.S. economy. As a result, the nation began to experience the worst inflation and unemployment rates since the Great Depression. To make matters worse, there was an oil embargo that ended the era of cheap energy in the U.S. Israel, and its Arab neighbors had fought the Yom Kippur War, and afterward, Arab oil-producing nations decided to punish the United States for helping Israel by cutting off U.S. oil imports. This caused gasoline prices to jump more than 70 percent.

Ford's wife, Betty, became an outspoken advocate of women's rights, supporting both liberalized abortion laws and the Equal Rights Amendment. Several opinion polls showed that Betty was more popular than her husband.

Ford's government was as open and simple as possible, and although he had never had any ambition to be president, he found that he enjoyed the job. He decided that rather than retire in 1976, he would run for a full term as president. Unfortunately for Ford, the nation's economy was still in a mess, and many people were out of work. While most people respected Ford, many wanted a president who could solve the problems of unemployment and inflation. Ford was defeated, and he retired to spend much of his time at sports such as golf and skiing.

JIMMY CARTER

39TH PRESIDENT: 1977 - 1981

Jimmy Carter's formal name is James Earl Carter Jr, but his family has always called him Jimmy. Even as president, he preferred to be called Jimmy. His father owned a farm and a small store in Georgia. He grew up wanting to be a sailor and was accepted by the U.S. Naval Academy. He graduated fifty-ninth in a class of 820. Two years after that, he was appointed to the nuclear submarine service.

He was twenty-nine when his father died. He resigned from the navy and returned home to run the family farm. He became a good businessman and grew the farm and bought a cotton gin. In 1955, the United States Supreme Court ruled that segregated schools were illegal. Many white people resented this, but Carter remembered riding to his all-white school on a bus while black children had to walk. This did not seem right in his eyes. He decided to run for the next country school board in order to try and work towards a peaceful solution to this issue. He was elected, and then he ran for the state senate and was also elected. In 1966, he ran for governor of Georgia but was defeated. He did not give up and ran for governor again in 1970, and this time he was elected.

He was not known outside of Georgia. When he set his eyes on the presidential candidacy, people asked, "Jimmy Who?" Even his mother was surprised when he told her of his plans to which she replied, "President of what?" Carter campaigned hard, traveling back and forth across the country, making speeches. Being an unknown played in his favor as many were still angry about the Nixon presidency, and anyone associated with Nixon was tainted. When Ford ran in the 1976 election, people did not want to vote for him since they wanted an outsider. Carter won the election and became the 39th President of the United States.

When President Carter took office, the nation's inflation rate was 6 percent. Prices were increasing at a rate of 6 percent every year, but salaries were remaining stagnant, so people's standard of living was being affected. Under Carter, this would get much worse and doubled to nearly 12 percent.

His biggest obstacle in solving the economic problems was the energy crisis. Oil prices kept going up, from fourteen dollars a barrel to twenty-eight dollars. This led to shortages of gasoline. Lines at the pumps sometimes reached more than a mile and half long, causing states to resort to gasoline rationing.

This led to a decline in auto manufacturers. People began buying smaller, more fuel-efficient Japanese cars rather than the gas-guzzling ones being made by U.S. companies. Three-hundred-thousand autoworkers lost their jobs, and more would have been fired if Congress had not approved more than a billion dollars in loan guarantees for Chrysler Automotive. To reduce America's dependence on foreign oil, Carter proposed an energy bill that included strict conservation rules as well as a fund to develop new energy sources.

During the late 1970s, some American's began opposing the construction of nuclear power plants. At first, their protest was small, but in 1977, fifteen hundred demonstrators were arrested when they tried to stop the construction of the Seabrook nuclear plant in New Hampshire. In March of 1979, an accident at the Three Mile Island plant outside of Harrisburg, Pennsylvania, awakened the public to the possible dangers of nuclear power. This resulted in sixty-five thousand people gathering in Washington to protest nuclear power. These protests halted plans to build a number of new facilities and led to improved safety at nuclear plants that continued to operate.

On November 4, 1979, a gang of Islamic students attacked the U.S. Embassy in Iran and took its staff hostage. Earlier that year, an Islamic revolution had toppled the U.S.-backed government. The student radicals in the embassy wanted to put their leader on trial for the crimes against their government. Their plan was to exchange the American hostages for the shah, who was then receiving cancer treatment in New York City.

President Carter did not approve of the torture that the shah had used to control Iran, but he also was not about to submit to terrorism. He tried to free the hostages through diplomatic efforts, but all of those efforts failed. As weeks and months passed, public pressure grew until Carter approved a military rescue plan. This mission failed when several helicopters crashed in a desert dust storm early in the attempts.

There was very little that Carter could do, but many people blamed him for both the economic problems and for allowing the hostages to remain imprisoned for more than a year. Carter did see some success in a different part of the Middle East. Egypt and Israel had been at war, off and on for many years. It was a dangerous situation that could erupt into a larger war involving the U.S. and the Soviet Union. President Carter invited the President of Egypt and Premier of Israel to visit him at Camp David near Washington, where the three men worked day after day with their advisers to draw up a fair peace treaty. Carter played a leading role in the negotiations, and the treaty was signed in March of 1979.

Carter remained unpopular in spite of this agreement. In 1980 an opinion poll showed that only 21 percent of the American people approved of Carter. It was the lowest rating any president had ever had in such a poll. When Carter ran for reelection, he was defeated by a landslide.

RONALD REAGAN

40TH PRESIDENT: 1981 - 1989

*A*s a child, Ronald Reagan lived in a number of small Illinois towns where his father was a shoe salesman. They never had much money, but that did not keep young Ronald from enjoying fishing and football. In high school, he was elected student body president and acted in school plays. Reagan went to Eureka College near his home and after getting a job at a radio station as a sports announcer. In 1937, when he was 26 years old, he moved to Hollywood and signed an acting contract with Warner Brothers studio.

During World War II, Reagan served in the Air Force. He was not in combat but made training films in California, and after the war, he turned to Hollywood. Until that time, he had been a Democrat, but as a member of the Screen Actors Guild, he became involved in a dispute between his union and other unions in the movie-making business. Some of the members had attended communist party meetings, and Reagan became convinced that communists were trying to take over the American Movie business.

Eventually, the dispute among the unions was settled, but Reagan remained certain that the Soviet Union was secretly trying to destroy noncommunist governments all over the world.

Reagan began working for the General Electric Company as a host on a series of television shows. He also traveled to General Electric plants and gave speeches to the workers and the management. He took on the thought that the government was becoming too big and was interfering with private business. He decided to leave the Democratic party and became a Republican. When Senator Barry Goldwater ran for president against Lyndon Johnson in the 1964 election, Reagan made speeches for Goldwater. Although Goldwater was defeated, Reagan's speeches made him very popular among the more conservative Republicans. In 1964, he was requested to run for governor, where he served two terms.

In 1968, while still governor, Reagan tried to get the Republican nomination for president, however, Nixon was nominated instead. In 1976, he tried again but lost to Gerald Ford. In 1980, Reagan tried a third time and was successful.

At that time, the country was having serious economic problems, and the cost of living was on the rise. Interest rates were so high; few people could afford to borrow money to buy new houses or start new businesses. Reagan promised to cut taxes and to save money by cutting government expenses. He also promised to build up the military to compete with Russia.

Reagan became known for his great speeches and was often called 'The Great Communicator.' He was elected by a wide margin becoming the 40th President of the United States. At 69 years old, he was also the oldest man ever to be elected.

Reagan kept his focus on the big picture as he was aware that presidents with too many proposals usually get nothing done. He concentrated on just a few ideas which were passed through Congress without a fight. Reagans' view was that all government spending was wasteful with the expectation of defense. He was quoted as saying, "Government is not the solution to our problems, government is the problem."

Reagan was able to lower taxes, raise defensive spending, and cut deeply into such social programs as food stamps and unemployment benefits. Social spending was better managed by the states.

When he took office, the inflation rate was over 13 percent, and there was slow economic growth. His plan to fix this was based on supply-side economics, which stated that increasing the amount of money in people's hands would increase both investment and demand, which would make the economy stronger. Reagan proposed a major tax cut for the rich because they were the people most likely to invest and spend. He told the public that, soon, the benefits of tax-cutting would "trickle-down" to everyone else. The income tax cut lowered individual rates by 25 percent over three years. As a result, rich people were indeed left with more money, but most didn't invest it. Instead, they spent it. Very little was left to trickle down to the middle class and even less to the poor. The economy continued to move deeper into the worst recession since World War II.

At the same time, the annual federal budget deficits spiked. The tax cut reduced revenues, and although billions were saved by cutting social programs, these savings were offset by larger increases in the defense budget. President Reagan often called on Congress to pass an amendment that required a balanced budget, but he never submitted a balanced budget himself. During his time in office, the national debt more than doubled, and interest payments on that debt became the third-largest federal spending item.

In a nationally televised speech, Reagan proposed that the United States build a space-based missile defense system that would use satellites to shoot down incoming nuclear misses to combat the Soviet Union, which he referred to as "the focus of evil in the modern world." The cost for it would be in the trillions of dollars, so it immediately became controversial on Capitol Hill and even adopted the name of 'Star Wars.' After Reagan's speech, scientists pointed out that the missile shield could not be built, but Reagan insisted on going ahead with his plan. He thought the best way to beat the Soviets was to outspend them.

In 1984 Reagan ran for a second term. Reagan kept reminding voters that under his administration, the rate of inflation had dropped sharply. Prices were still going up but not nearly as rapidly as a few years before. Interest rates were still high but much lower than they had been. On the whole, the economy had improved. Because of Reagan's increased military spending with no new taxes, the country was going deeper into debt. The 1984 federal budget deficit was estimated at more than $180 billion. Despite this, Reagan was reelected. Early in his second term, Reagan had to go to the hospital to have a cancerous tumor removed. He quickly recovered.

In March 1985, Mikhail Gorbachev came to power in the Soviet Union. Gorbachev realized that his country could not afford to match the U.S. arms buildup, and their economy would lag unless they made serious changes. Gorbachev began to ease tensions with the United States by helping to wind down the Cold War. In December of 1987, he and Reagan signed the Intermediate-Range Nuclear Forces agreement, which was an agreement between the two superpowers to reduce the number of nuclear warheads in their arsenals.

Reagan acted quickly and firmly to the increasing terrorist attacks around the world. In April 1986, he ordered airstrikes against military targets in Libya, after confirming that the Libyan leader, Colonel Muammar al-Qaddafi, had been behind many terrorist attacks against the U.S.

When Reagan requested more money to support the rebel Contra forces fighting the pro-communist regime in Nicaragua, Congress resisted. They thought it would mean getting involved in another Vietnam. Reagan refused to give up and also refused to abandon the Americans kidnapped by terrorists in Beirut, believing that Iran was actually behind the kidnappings.

He had stated many times he would make no bargains to secure the release of hostages, so it came as a great shock when a Beirut magazine was reporting in November of 1986 that former National Security Adviser had been in Iran negotiating an arms shipment. It was even more shocking to learn that the arms had been shipped to secure the release of the kidnapped Americans. Profits from the sales had been diverted to the Contras in Nicaragua.

This grew into a national scandal. Congress set up special committees to investigate. Reagan was cleared of any direct involvement, but it was obvious he had let his staff get out of hand.

In early October of 1987, the value of U.S. stocks plunged. Reagan's financial policies were in trouble, and the increasing social and military spending had resulted in huge budget deficits. The United States was now the biggest debtor nation in the world.

By the time Reagan left office, the stock market was performing well. People talked less about the Iran-Contra ordeal and more about the improved relations with the Soviet Union. According to the polls, Reagan was one of the most popular presidents in many years.

GEORGE BUSH

41ST PRESIDENT: 1989 - 1993

George Herbert Walker Bush was named after his maternal grandfather, George Herbert Walker. His grandfather Walker established the Walker Cup, a trophy awarded every two years to the winners in team matches between American and British amateur men golfers.

George grew up in Greenwich, Connecticut, but his family spent their summers at the Walker vacation home in Maine. Young George loved fishing, boating, and being out at sea. When he was nine, he and his brother took a boat out on the Atlantic Ocean by themselves.

He graduated from Phillips Academy, and a few days later, he went to Boston to be sworn into the U.S.

Navy. He received preflight training in North Carolina, and became one of the US Navy's youngest pilots when he received his Naval Aviator wings three days before turning 19.

On September 2, 1944, he took part in a bombing mission against Japanese bases in southeast Japan when he and his two crew members had to bail out with parachutes due to Japanese anti-aircraft guns. While floating on a life raft, a U.S. submarine rescued him. The other two men were never found. For his heroism, Bush was awarded the Distinguished Flying Cross.

Bush then went on to enroll in Yale University, along with his wife, Barbara. He majored in economics and was elected to Phi Beta Kappa, a national honor society whose members are chosen for academic excellence. During his senior year, he was made captain of the Yale baseball team.

After graduation, Bush moved to Texas because he wanted to get into the oil business, which was booming. He joined some friends in the founding of two oil companies. His success made him very wealthy, but his true calling was going into politics. His father, Prescott Bush, had served as a senator from Connecticut for ten years.

He ran as the Texas Republican candidate for the House of Representatives and won. He went on to run for the Senate but ultimately lost. Soon after his defeat, President Nixon appointed Bush as the United States ambassador to the United Nations. This gave Bush his first taste of international politics. He was then asked to take over as Chairman of the Republican National Committee. It was during this time that the Watergate news broke, which lead to Nixon's resignation.

When President Ford replaced Nixon, he appointed Bush to be the nation's chief diplomatic representative to China. Later, Ford called Bush back to Washington to become Director of the Central Intelligence Agency. He served as director for two years, trying to restore the credibility that it had lost during Vietnam as well as Watergate.

After Ford lost his bid for re-election, Bush decided that he would be a candidate for the next election. He lost the nomination to Ronald Reagan, but Reagan chose Bush to be his vice president. Bush and President Reagan had regular weekly lunch meetings, and Reagan delegated many responsibilities to Vice President Bush. Since he had access to so much, this made him the obvious candidate to succeed Reagan, and in 1988 he won the Republican nomination. He was successful in his campaign, and he became the 41st President of the United States.

He ran on a platform of free trade and continued American leadership in world affairs. He worked to set up new trade agreements that would enable foreign governments to sell their products in the United States and American businesses to sell abroad. One of the promises he made to voters was "No new taxes."

The forty-year struggle between the U.S. and the Soviet Union ended during President Bush's presidency. In December of 1988, Soviet leader Mikhail Gorbachev declared in a speech to the United Nations that the Cold War was over. He followed that up by undertaking reforms at home like reducing the presence of Soviet troops in Eastern Europe and later removing them altogether. One by one, the communist governments of Eastern Europe were driven from power. On October 3, 1990, East and West Germany were reunited into one country after the Berlin Wall was taken down.

At first, President Bush tried to work with Gorbachev to improve relations between the two countries, but in August of 1990, Gorbachev was driven from power. By the end of the year, the Soviet Union had fallen apart, and Bush now had to work with Boris Yeltsin, President of the Republic of Russia.

Bush shifted his focus to Panama, which was ruled by dictator Manuel Noriega. Under the Reagan administration, the CIA had allowed Noriega to smuggle drugs because he gave the U.S. important intelligence information. Noriega started delivering more and more anti-American speeches, and President Bush had enough.

At first, President Bush imposed economic sanctions and encouraged Noriega's rivals to overthrow him. When neither of the tactics worked, he ordered military action. Twelve thousand soldiers invaded Panama, where Noriega was captured and flown to Florida to stand trial on drug charges.

A year later, Iraqi troops invaded the Persian Gulf nation of Kuwait. Although it was a small country, it was responsible for about 10 percent of the world's oil reserves. If Iraqi dictator Saddam Hussein were able to conquer Saudi Arabia as well, he would control nearly half of the world's oil. The U.N. Security Council voted to impose economic sanctions and gave member nations permission to enforce them with military means. Even the Soviet Union, who was Saddam Hussein's largest weapons supplier, stopped selling to Iraq.

Bush began sending U.S. troops to defend Saudi Arabia, eventually sending more than half a million American soldiers there as part of Operation Desert Shield (phase 1 - the preparation phase). Other countries like Great Britain, France, Egypt, and Syria all joined in as well.

In November of 1990, the Security Council set a deadline of January 15 for a complete withdrawal of Iraqi troops from Kuwait. If they did not oblige, U.N. member nations could use force. Seven hours after the deadline passed, Bush began Operation Desert Storm (phase 2 - the combat phase).

During the next six weeks, bombers began devastating the Iraqi military. After that, the ground assault began, and in less than 100 hours, the Iraqi army was overrun, and Kuwait was liberated. After the war, Bush became extremely popular in the U.S. This was an important military victory, and he proved that he could handle himself well in an international crisis. It appeared that he would win a second term with ease, but problems were building up at home. Savings and loan (S&L) associations, which were financial institutions similar to a bank that would specialize in providing checking, savings, loans and residential mortgages to consumers, had been allowed to use their depositors' money to make risky loans and investments. Since the government-insured savings deposits, it had to pay back the depositors when the investments went bad, and the S&Ls no longer had the money. As one large S&L after another went broke, the cost to the taxpayers mounted into the billions. Bush's son, Neil, had been a director at one of the failed S&Ls.

The boom of the Reagan years was over, and in came an economic recession and was one of the deepest in decades. Businesses went bankrupt at alarming rates, and about ten million Americans were out of work. The federal government had tripled the national debt during the Reagan years, and now the recession made it impossible balance the budget again.

Many of these problems were not Bush's fault, as it had been set in motion well before he took office. When it came to dealing with troubles at home, the president seemed like a different person from the strong leader who had handled foreign affairs. He had few bold ideas at home in America and was often unable to get Congress to cooperate.

As early as 1990, Bush was forced to break his promise to the voters by asking Congress to pass new taxes. He also had a strong stance that abortions should be against the law, which caused a divide among the supporters of both parties.

Campaigning for re-election in 1992, Bush faced an uphill battle. A wealthy Texan named Ross Perot ran as an independent and focused much of his attention and criticism on Bush and his lack of planning to cut the national debt. Even though Perot had no chance of winning, his attacks on Bush had an effect. In the end, the voters decided it was time for a change, and Bush lost the re-election.

BILL CLINTON

42ND PRESIDENT: 1993 - 2001

*S*imilar to President Gerald Ford, Bill Clinton started with another name. At his birth, he was named after his father, William Jefferson Blythe, who was a traveling salesman that had recently died in an automobile accident. Bill's mother, Virginia, worked as a nurse to support herself and her son. When Bill was four, she married again. Her new husband, Roger Clinton, adopted Bill, who then changed his last name to Clinton.

Bill grew up in Hot Springs, Arkansas. He did not have an easy home life as his stepfather was an alcoholic and sometimes became violent when drunk. He once fired off a gun during a family fight, and the police threw him in jail. Virginia Clinton divorced her second husband but quickly married him again.

Most of Bill's classmates knew nothing about these problems. He was a good student who attended the Baptist Church and loved gospel music. He spent hours practicing the saxophone. His favorite artists were Elvis Presley and James Brown.

Even as a boy, Clinton loved politics. He ran for so many class and club offices that his principal barred him from campaigning for any more. In 1963, he visited Washington D.C. and shook hands with President John F. Kennedy at the White House. Clinton knew that someday he wanted to be president.

When he graduated high school, he was offered several music scholarships. Instead, he chose to attend Georgetown University in Washington, D.C. He majored in political science, and during his senior year, he had a summer job as an aide to the Chairman of the Foreign Relations Committee. At the time this powerful committee was header by Senator J William Fulbright of Arkansas. This senator was one of the few nationally known Arkansas politicians, and he became Bill Clinton's hero and role model.

After graduation, Clinton won a Rhodes scholarship, enabling him to spend two years at Oxford University in England. He then went to Yale Law School, where he met his future wife, Hillary Rodham.

In 1973, Clinton returned home to Arkansas to teach at the University of Arkansas Law School, and a year later, he ran for Congress. He lost but only narrowly. In 1978, he ran for and was elected Governor of Arkansas. He was only thirty-two, which made him the youngest governor in the nation.

Clinton lost the favor of the people in Arkansas because it seemed he was already running for President and saw his job as a brief stop along the way. In 1980, he was defeated in a bid for re-election. Two years later, he tried again more humbly this time and asked the people of Arkansas for a second chance. "I learned my lesson," he said in a speech. He won the election and went on to become one of the county's most popular and long-serving governors.

Governor Clinton entered the 1992 presidential race as a middle-of-the-road candidate. He called for the government to invest more money in improving schools, roads, and public services. He emphasized the need for more job training so that the unemployed could find work in other industries, and he proposed a plan that would enable all Americans to have access to health insurance. While President Bush talked about trust and experience, the majority of voters were worried about the economy and ready to take a chance on a new approach. Bill Clinton was elected as the 42nd President of the United States and became the first president that was born after World War II.

During his first two years in office, the president had some difficulties with the Democrats in Congress, but he was able to win two important trade battles. In November of 1993, the House approved the North American Free Trade Agreement (NAFTA), which created a free-trade zone linking the U.S., Mexico, and Canada. A year later, Congress ratified the General Agreement on Tariffs and Trade.

Due to budget concerns and difficulties, a partial shutdown of the federal government took place. Offices were closed, and eight hundred thousand workers were sent home. The shutdown lasted six days when President Clinton accepted the Republican goal of balancing the budget within seven years.

There was also trouble abroad that Clinton needed to address early on. In the former Yugoslavia,

Serbians, Croatians, and Bosnian Muslims were fighting the bloodiest war in Europe since World War II. The Serbs wanted to carve out the independent state of Bosnia, an ethnically pure Serbian homeland. Over four years of fighting, 250,000 people died.

With the budget crisis at home taking most of his time, President Clinton brought the warring factions together at an air force base in Dayton, Ohio. After three weeks of tense negotiations, the three parties finally agreed on a peace plan.

President Clinton agreed to send twenty thousand troops to Bosnia to help guarantee peace. These soldiers policed Bosnia as part of a ninety-thousand-soldier U.N. Implementation Force. The Dayton peace plan, which preserved the unity of Bosnia, called for limited disarmament to be followed by free elections.

However, Serbian president Slobodan Milosevic continued to act aggressively elsewhere in the Balkans. Since he lost control in Bosnia, he turned his attention to Kosovo, a province in southern Serbia where nine out of ten residents were ethnic Albanians. This escalated into violence as Christian

Serb security forces began "cleansing" Kosovo of its many Muslim Albanian citizens.

The Serbian violence became so brutal that in 1998, NATO issued an ultimatum to Milosevic, threatening air strikes unless he immediately stopped the rampaging. Milosevic withdrew just enough troops to delay the bombings. Negotiations continued for several months until NATO issued another ultimatum. This time, neither side backed down, and NATO began an eleven-week aerial offensive, which was the first NATO military operation ever mounted against a sovereign country.

Clinton now had to worry about the Russians, who were allies of the Serbs, and who strongly opposed NATO's strong-arm tactics. Russia was also experiencing a difficult transition from Communism to multiparty democracy, and its military was on the decline. This still posed a possibility of Russia interceding on Serbia's behalf, if only to boost its own sinking morale and divert attention away from its economic issues.

Due to Boris Yeltsin's close ties to President Clinton, the State Department was able to enlist Yeltsin's help in pressuring Milosevic to concede, and on June 9, the war in Kosovo ended.

President Clinton was able to commit his time and energy to make peace around the world because, at home, the economy was booming. An indication of the good times was the persistent rise in stock prices. Low unemployment, low inflation, and high productivity, along with earlier government belt-tightening, eliminated the budget deficits.

In February of 1998, Clinton proposed the first balanced budget since 1969, and a year later, the government was running a surplus, meaning its income from taxes and fees exceeded the amount it spent on programs and interest payments on the national debt.

The only issue the President seemed to be having was the Whitewater investigation. It started after his inauguration and continued until the end of his second term. Kenneth Star's investigation into Clinton led to new charges that the president had lied under oath to conceal an intimate relationship he had had with a young White House staff member, Monica Lewinsky.

For months after the story broke, Clinton denied the affair. On August 17, evidence forced him to admit that he had been misleading people. He apologized, but few Americans were satisfied because they believed that his apology was insincere and intended only to break the gathering momentum for impeachment. The Senate later decided to acquit him of the charges.

GEORGE W. BUSH
43RD PRESIDENT: 2001 - 2009

George Walker Bush was born in New Haven, Connecticut. His father and future President George Herbert Walker Bush was attending Yale University at the time after he was discharged from the Navy. When George was two years old, the family moved to western Texas, where his father had accepted a job in the oil business. George W. attended school in Midland before being sent back east to Phillips Academy in Massachusetts. He went on to attend Yale University, just like his father. During this time, Bush was a cheerleader as well as a member of the Delta Kappa Epsilon, serving as the president of the fraternity during his senior year. Bush entered Harvard Business School in the fall of 1973. He graduated in 1975 with an MBA. George W. Bush was the only U.S. president to have earned an MBA at the time.

While in school, Bush was less known for his good work habits and more for his partying. This continued well into his thirties until the middle of the 1980s when he joined a men's Bible study group and became a born-again Christian. His heavy drinking had been a strain on his marriage, but he put that behind him when he gave up alcohol shortly after his fortieth birthday.

In May 1968, Bush was commissioned into the Texas Air National Guard. After two years of training in active-duty service, he was assigned to Houston, flying Convair F-102s with the 147th Reconnaissance Wing.

In 1977, Bush established Arbusto Energy, a small oil exploration company, and later changed the name to Bush Exploration. In 1984, his company merged with the larger Spectrum 7, and Bush became chairman. Decreased oil prices hurt the company, and it folded into HKN, Inc., with Bush becoming a member of HKN's board of directors.

In 1978, Bush ran for the House of Representatives from Texas's 19th congressional district. Bush's opponent, Kent Hance, portrayed him as out of touch with rural Texans, and Bush lost the election with 46.8 percent of the vote. Bush and his family moved to Washington, D.C., in 1988 to work on his father's campaign for the U.S. presidency. He served as a campaign advisor and liaison to the media, and assisted his father by campaigning across the country.

In April 1989, Bush arranged for a group of investors to purchase a controlling interest in the Texas Rangers baseball franchise for $89 million and invested $500,000 himself. He served as managing general partner for five years. He led the team's projects and consistently attended its games, often choosing to sit amongst the fans. Bush's sale of his shares in the Rangers in 1998 net him over $15 million from his initial $500,000 investment.

In 1994, Bush declared his candidacy to be Governor of Texas gubernatorial election at the same time that his brother Jeb sought the governorship of Florida. After easily winning the Republican primary, Bush faced popular Democratic incumbent Governor Ann Richards. In the course of the campaign, Bush pledged to sign a bill allowing Texans to obtain permits to carry concealed weapons. Richards had vetoed the bill, but Bush signed it into law after he became governor. In 1998, Bush won re-election with a record 69 percent of the vote. He became the first governor in Texas history to be elected to two consecutive four-year terms.

Bush was the Governor of Texas in June 1999 when he announced his candidacy for President of the United States. He campaigned on a platform that included bringing integrity and honor back to the White House, increasing the size of the United States Armed Forces, cutting taxes, improving education, and aiding minorities. By early 2000, the race was down to Bush and John McCain. On July 25, 2000, Bush surprised some observers when he selected Dick Cheney—a former White House Chief of Staff, U.S. Representative, and Secretary of Defense—to be his running mate. At the time, Cheney was serving as head of Bush's vice-presidential search committee. Soon after, at the 2000 Republican National Convention, Bush and Cheney were officially nominated by the Republican Party.

When the election votes were tallied on November 7, Bush had won 29 states, including Florida. The closeness of the Florida outcome led to a recount.

The initial recount also went to Bush, but the outcome was tied up in lower courts for a month until eventually reaching the U.S. Supreme Court. On December 9, in the controversial Bush v. Gore ruling, the Court reversed a Florida Supreme Court decision that had ordered a third count and stopped an ordered statewide hand recount based on the argument that the use of different standards among Florida's counties violated the Equal Protection Clause of the Fourteenth Amendment. The machine recount showed that Bush had won the Florida vote by a margin of 537 votes out of six million casts. Although he had received 543,895 fewer individual nationwide votes than Gore, Bush won the election, making him the 43rd President of the United States. Bush was the first person to win an American presidential election with fewer popular votes than another candidate since Benjamin Harrison in 1888.

Due to the controversy of how he had won the election, Bush took office over a deeply divided nation. As a candidate, he had described himself as a conservative who could bring people together. As a president, however, he relied primarily on a small circle of close advisers. From the start, he governed with a strong sense of moral certainty that pleased Americans who shared his deep religious faith.

Under President Clinton, Congress had shifted the tax burden from the bottom 80 percent to the top 1 percent of the population. Two weeks after taking office, President Bush proposed spending the large budget surplus that Clinton's economic policies had generated on a ten-year, $1.6 trillion tax cut. This would mean that 43 percent of the tax cut would go to the richest 1 percent of Americans. He believed the money belonged to the American taxpayers, and they should get to keep it.

At around eight o'clock in the morning on September 11, 2001, nineteen men belonging to the Islamic terrorist group al-Qaeda seized control of four airborne passenger jets. At 8:46 am, one of those planes crashed into the North Tower of the World Trade Center in New York City. Soon, another plane hit the South Tower, and then a third plane was flown into the Pentagon outside of Washington, D.C. The fourth jet never reached its target, which most expected to be the White House or the Capitol. Learning from cell phone conversations what had already happened, passengers on board that plane stormed the cockpit and forced the jet to crash in rural Pennsylvania, killing everyone on board. Altogether, three thousand people died in the 9/11 attacks.

The nation had not received such a shocking blow since the Japanese bombing of Pearl Harbor in 1941. Bush promised to lead the nation in a "war on terrorism" that would rid the world of evildoers. This theme became central to Bush's policies and left little room for differences of opinion. "Every nation in every region now has a decision to make," going on to say, "Either you are with us, or you are with the terrorists."

The first battlefield in the war on terror was Afghanistan. The Taliban government had been sheltering Osama Bin Laden, President Bush's plan to dispose of the Taliban received a great deal of international support. On October 7, 2001, the United States and British bombers began attacking targets inside Afghanistan. The forces of the rebel Northern Alliance soon removed the Taliban from power and established a new pro-Western government.

At home, President Bush began reorganizing his administration around the war on terrorism. He supported the creation of a new Department of Homeland Security, which brought together 17,000 workers from twenty-two different agencies. This was the most far-reaching rearrangement of the federal government since the 1940s. President Bush also backed the USA Patriot Act, which granted sweeping new powers to law enforcement agencies at the expense of some civil liberties. The act expanded the federal government's ability to intercept e-mails, search financial and other records as well as detain people.

He also authorized the National Security Agency to begin eavesdropping on the telephone conversations of suspected terrorists without obtaining the necessary warrants from the court. Many described this as illegal, but members of Congress passed a new law authorizing a similar program.

The Bush administration made plans to invade Iraq after declaring that it was a threat to the United States. Bush stated that their dictator, Saddam Hussein, had weapons of mass destruction, and he also had strong ties to al-Qaeda. Many of America's closest European and Asian allies disagreed. Since the end of the 1991 Persian Gulf War, U.N. inspectors had been searching for evidence that Iraq possessed weapons of mass destruction, but no evidence was ever found.

Despite their resistance, Bush moved ahead with his doctrine, stating that the United States could attack a country that is considered a threat to its national security, even if that country had not yet attacked the United States. Congress authorized the use of military force in Iraq.

On March 19, 2003, The U.S. went to war with Iraq. Aided by the British, U.S. troops captured the Iraqi capital of Baghdad and scattered Saddam Hussein's army in about six weeks. On May 1, President Bush declared victory in Iraq. However, the fighting didn't end. It only got worse, and over the next five years, Iraqi resistance fighters staged ambushes and car bombing that killed more than four thousand American soldiers. The death toll among Iraqi civilians was about twenty times higher. During 2004 and 2005, the President's handling of the war came under scrutiny. Americans began to realize that he hadn't thought through what to do with Iraq once Saddam Hussein was removed from power. The U.S. failed to deploy enough troops to establish law and order in Iraq. The civilian officials who were appointed to govern occupied Iraq knew little about the region and even less about how to defeat an insurgency. Also, many corrupt American and Iraqi companies stole billions of dollars in reconstruction funds.

As part of the war on terrorism, President Bush used his power to imprison hundreds of people at Guantanamo Bay, Cuba. While claiming that those people were terrorists, few were ever charged with a crime or allowed to defend themselves in court. They were held for years and interrogated using methods that many people considered to be torture. The Bush administration argued that because Guantanamo prisoners were being held on Cuban soil, they were outside the jurisdiction of American judges. In June 2004, the Supreme Court ruled that all prisoners being held at Guantanamo Bay had to be given access to U.S. courts.

By 2006, the war in Iraq had become very unpopular, and it prompted the Democratic Party to make it the central focus of the new campaign. Most Democratic candidates promised to end the war quickly and bring the troops home. President Bush realized that he would have to change strategies, but rather than bringing the troops home, he decided to send more troops to Iraq.

He called his new policy a "troop surge." He determined that deploying additional troops would reduce the violence, allowing Iraqis to reach the political settlement that everyone agreed was needed for lasting peace. The result of the surge was mixed and because violence in Iraq declined, most people considered the surge a success. However, the purpose of the surge had been to resolve Iraq's political problems, and this did not happen.

While continuing to be faulted for mishandling the Iraq War, President Bush was also strongly criticized during his second term for the way he ran the federal government. The poor performance of the Federal Emergency Management Agency during the 2005 Hurricane Katrina crisis called attention to some of the people he had appointed to high-paying federal jobs.

In December 2006, Attorney General Alberto Gonzales fired nine U.S. Attorneys. A congressional investigation later determined that these U.S. Attorneys, whose job it was to prosecute federal crimes, had been dismissed because the president's political advisers didn't think they were partisan enough. Although strongly defended by President Bush, Gonzales and several other Justice Department officials were forced to resign.

BARACK OBAMA

44TH PRESIDENT: 2009 - 2013

Obama's father, Barack Obama Sr., was born in Kenya, where he grew up herding goats and later earned a scholarship that allowed him to leave and pursue a college education in Hawaii. While studying at the University of Hawaii, Obama Sr. met Ann Dunham, where they eventually married, and six months later, on August 4, 1961, had Barack Hussein Obama II. As a child, Obama did not have a relationship with his father. Obama's parents divorced when he was two, and his father eventually returned to Kenya.

Obama grew up in Hawaii with his grandparents after his mom moved to Indonesia. While living with his grandparents, Obama went to school at Punahou Academy. He was one of only three black students, so he learned about racism from an early age.

He went on to attend Occidental College in Los Angeles in 1979. After two years, he transferred to Columbia University in New York City, where he earned a degree in political science. He moved to Chicago in 1985 to work on the South Side as a community organizer for low-income residents. In 1991, he graduated magna cum laude from Harvard Law. He was elected the first African American editor of the *Harvard Law Review*.

After law school, he returned to Chicago to practice as a civil rights lawyer. He also taught constitutional law part-time at the University of Chicago Law School. He ran for a seat in the Illinois State Senate in 1996, where he won and went on to draft legislation on health care services and childhood education programs for the poor. In 2000, he made an unsuccessful Democratic primary run for the House of Representatives. After his loss, he created a campaign committee and began raising funds to run for a seat in the Senate in 2004, which he won.

In 2007, Obama announced his candidacy for the 2008 Presidential campaign. He was locked in a tight battle with former first lady Hillary Clinton for the

Democratic nomination. After securing a sufficient number of pledges, he won the nomination. On November 4, 2008, Obama defeated Republican presidential nominee John McCain to become the 44th President of the United States. He was also the first African American to become president.

When he took office, he inherited a global recession, two ongoing wars, and the lowest international favorability rating for the United States. He campaigned on financial reform and reinventing education and health care. He hit the ground running, and within his first 100 days, he was able to convince Congress to expand health care insurance for children and provide legal protection for women seeking equal pay. Also, a $787 billion stimulus bill was passed to promote economic growth. Housing and credit markets were assisted with a plan to buy U.S. bank's toxic assets. Also, loans were made to the auto industry to keep their operations afloat, and stricter regulations were put on Wall Street. He also cut taxes for working families, small businesses, and first-time home buyers.

He undertook a complete overhaul of America's foreign policy by reaching out to improve relations with Europe, China, and Russia. He lobbied U.S.

allies to support a global economic stimulus package. He also agreed to send over 21,000 troops to Afghanistan as well as setting an August 2010 date for the withdrawal of U.S. troops from Iraq.

On April 29, 2011, Obama approved a covert operation in Pakistan to track down the leader responsible for the attacks on the United States on September 11. Osama bin Laden had been in hiding for nearly ten years. On May 2, U.S. Navy Seal Team Six raided a compound in Abbottabad, Pakistan, and within 40 minutes, killed bin Laden. There were no American casualties, and the team was able to collect invaluable information about the inner-workings of al-Qaeda.

On that same day, Obama announced on national television the death of Osama bin Laden. "For over two decades, bin Laden has been al Qaeda's leader and symbol and has continued to plot attacks against our country and our friends and allies. The death of bin Laden marks the most significant achievement to date in our nation's effort to defeat al Qaeda."

President Obama found himself in an international crisis in late August of 2013. It was discovered that the Syrian leader had used chemical weapons against civilians. Thousands of people, including over 400 children, had been killed in the chemical attacks. The president worked to convince Congress and the international community to take action against Syria but was met with resistance from Capitol Hill. They did not want to get involved and take military action. Obama had an alternative plan stating that if the Syrian leader agreed with the stipulation made by Russia to give up its chemical weapons, the direct strike against the nation would not take place. The Syrian leader acknowledged possession of the chemical weapons and accepted the Russian proposal.

Despite opposition from Congressional Republicans and the populist Tea Party movement, Obama signed his health care reform plan into law in March of 2010. Known as the Affordable Care Act, it prohibited the denial of coverage based on pre-existing conditions, allowed citizens under 26 years old to be insured under parental plans, provided for free health screening for certain citizens and expanded insurance coverage and access to medical care for millions of Americans. He gained a legal victory in June of 2012 when the U.S. Supreme Court upheld the Affordable Care Act's individual mandate, which required citizens to purchase health insurance or pay a tax. Opponents of the Affordable Care Act said that it added new costs to the country's overblown budget, violated the Constitution with its requirement for individuals to obtain insurance, and amounted to a "government takeover" of health care. In October of 2013, a dispute over the federal budget caused a 16-day shutdown of the federal government. The Affordable Care Act continued to come under fire in October after the failed launch of HealthCare.gov, the website meant to allow people to purchase health insurance online.

After leaving the White House, the Obama family moved to a home in Washington, D.C., to allow their youngest daughter to continue school. Obama embarked on a three-nation tour in the fall of 2017, meeting with heads of state in China and India. He remains active in politics to this day, delivering speeches across the country.

DONALD TRUMP

45TH PRESIDENT: 2017 - 2021

Donald Trump was born in Queens, New York, in 1946 to a wealthy real estate developer named Frederick Trump and his wife, Mary. He was an energetic child that grew up in the 1950s when the Trumps' wealth increased with the postwar real estate boom. At 13 years old, Trump's parents sent him to the New York Military Academy, hoping the discipline would channel his energy in a positive manner. He did well and graduated in 1964. He attended Fordham University and then transferred to the Wharton School of Finance at the University of Pennsylvania and graduated with a degree in economics. During his college years, he worked at his father's real estate business during the summer.

He followed his father into business as a real estate developer. His business ventures include The Trump Organization, Trump Tower, the Plaza Hotel, casinos in Atlantic City, and television franchises like *The Apprentice, Miss Universe and Miss USA*. He has written over 14 books, his first book *The Art of the Deal* published in 1987.

Trump announced his candidacy on June 16, 2015 and accepted the Republican nomination in July of 2016 against Democrat Hillary Clinton. In his campaign speeches, he outlined the issues he aimed to work on as president, including American violence, economic issues, immigration, trade, and terrorism. His campaign slogan was, "Make America Great Again."

He also promised supporters that he would renegotiate trade deals, reduce taxes and government regulations, repeal the Affordable Care Act (otherwise known as Obamacare), defend Second Amendment gun rights, and rebuild our depleted military.

Trump won the elector votes making him the 45th President of the United States and was sworn into office in 2017. In the first days of his presidency, Trump issued a number of back-to-back executive orders to make good on some of his campaign promises, as well as several orders aimed at rolling back policies and regulations that were put into place during the Obama administration.

In 2017, Trump signed an order to ban travel from seven Muslin-majority nations. He also notified member countries of the U.S. withdrawal from the Trans-Pacific Partnership free trade deal. In May, Trump fired FBI chief James Comey, national security adviser Michael Flynn, and attorney general Sally Yates. In June, he announced the U.S. exit from the Paris climate pact. In July, Trump began to travel the world and meet other leaders including Japan's Shinzo Abe and Russian President Vladimir Putin for the first time as president. Trump warns North Korea that they will face "fire and fury" amid nuclear and missile threats. In November, Trump had his first visit to Japan, South Korea, China, Vietnam, and the Philippines as president introducing the "Indo-Pacific" as a new way of engaging the region. Trump also overturned U.S. policy on the Israeli-Palestinian conflict by recognizing Jerusalem as Israel's capital. Trump signed the Tax Cuts and Jobs Act (TCJA) in December which cut individual income tax rates, doubled the standard deduction, and eliminated personal exemptions from the tax code, which expire the end of 2025 unless Congress acts to renew some or all of the provisions. The TCJA also cut the corporate tax rate from 35% to 21% effective in 2018 as well and these corporate cuts are permanent.

In 2018, Trump announced the U.S. withdrawal from the Iran nuclear deal and decided to reimpose sanctions on the country. He met with the North Korean leader Kim Jong Un in Singapore, which is the first-ever summit between the two countries. Their joint declaration stressed cooperation to include the complete denuclearization of the Korean Peninsula. The U.S. and China started a tariff war with tariffs of between 30-50% on Chinese steel and aluminum and tariffs on U.S. imports from China and Beijing as well. Trump administration's national defense strategy throughout his term stands out as one of the most important defense policy shifts of the last generation, refocusing the American military to confront the rising and increasingly aggressive powers of Russia and China. In November, the Democratic Party regained the majority in the House of Representatives, while Republican Party retained a majority in Senate in the midterm elections. Also in 2018 a zero-tolerance policy at the border with Mexico was enforced for illegal immigrants.

In 2019, Trump wanted $5.7 billion for a wall along the southern U.S. border which resulted in a congressional battle that ended after a 35-day shutdown of the federal government. Trump also announced the U.S. withdrawal from the Intermediate Range Nuclear Forces Treaty with Russia. In June, Trump becomes the first sitting U.S. president to step into North Korea when he met Kim Jong Un at the demilitarized zone diving the two Koreas. In October, the U.S. and Japan sign a trade deal at the White House. Trump also announces that the leader of the self-proclaimed Islamic State in Iraq and Syria, Abu Bark al-Baghdadi, has been killed by U.S. forces, eight months after ISIS lost the last territory of its caliphate in Syria. In December, the Democratic majority House brought charges for impeachment against Trump which he is found not guilty for by the U.S. Senate.

In 2020, the U.S. military killed top Iranian General Qassem Soleimani in a drone strike in Iraq. Soleimani was the commander of the Iranian Islamic Revolutionary Guard Cops elite Quds Force and was linked to violent demonstrations at the U.S. embassy in Baghdad and to the deaths of hundreds of American and allied troops in the region. In the beginning of the year, the U.S. and China signed a partial trade deal at the White House. In March, 2020 Trump declared a national emergency over the outbreak of the coronavirus (COVID-19). The declaration opened access to $50 billion in emergency funding. He later signed more than $2 trillion in economic stimulus. In May, black man George Floyd died in police custody in Minnesota, which sparked nationwide anti-racism protests. In July, U.S. notified the United Nations of its withdrawal from the World Health Organization because Trump Administration says it had been misleading the world about COVID-19 under pressure from China. Trump also signed an order to end U.S. preferential treatment for Hong Kong. U.S. Secretary of State Mike Pompeo announced the end of decades-old "blind-engagement" with China and the U.S. closes the Chinese consulate in Houston. The U.S. Health Secretary traveled to Taiwan, which is the highest-level visit by a U.S. Cabinet official in over four decades. The Senate confirms Trump's Supreme Court nominee Amy Coney Barrett as a conservative justice replacing Ruth Bader Ginsburg.

Leading up to the 2020 U.S. presidential election the tension between Republican and Democratic parties continued and there was widespread distrust of the media by the general public. President Trump ran against Democratic Party nominee Joe Biden as presidential candidate. It was an extremely close election in November with the highest proportion of adult participation in the election in U.S. history. The Associated Press declared the election for Joe Biden. Trump voiced concerns about voter fraud and Texas Attorney General Ken Paxton took it to the Supreme Court regarding the voter count in four controversial states - Pennsylvania, Michigan, Wisconsin, and Georgia. The Supreme Court declined to hear the Paxton lawsuit. The electoral college then met to cast their votes in December and in January Joe Biden was declared the winner of the 2020 presidential election.

Printed in Great Britain
by Amazon